EXPLORE JERSEY
ITS COAST, COUNTRYSIDE AND HERITAGE

BETH LLOYD

Photographs by Gary Grimshaw

LOCAL HERITAGE BOOKS

Front cover photograph = North Coast Cliff Walk
Back cover photograph = The Elms Farm, St. Mary

EXPLORE JERSEY
Its Coast, Countryside and Heritage
by Beth Lloyd

First Published 1984
© Beth Lloyd 1984
Revised and reprinted 1985

LOCAL HERITAGE BOOKS
3, Catherine Road, Newbury,
Berkshire
and 36 Queens Road, Newbury,
Berkshire

Designed by Ray Hyden
Typesetting and Artwork: Type Generation Ltd. London
Sketch maps by Jean Le Boutillier
Produced through
MRM (Print Consultants) Ltd. Baughurst, Hampshire
Printed and bound in Great Britain by the
Guernsey Press Co. Ltd, Guernsey, Channel Islands.

ISBN 0 86368 007 0

BIBLIOGRAPHY

The Bailiwick of Jersey – G. R. Balleine
Balleine's History of Jersey – Marguerite Syvret
    and Joan Stevens
The Channel Islands – An Archaeological Guide –
    David E. Johnston
Jersey Folk Lore – John H. L'Amy
Old Jersey Houses – Joan Stevens
A Short History of Jersey – Joan Stevens
A Natural History of Jersey – Frances Le Sueur
Buildings and Memorials of the Channel Islands –
    Raoul Lemprière
Portrait of the Channel Islands – Raoul Lemprière
Walks for Motorists: Jersey – F. de L. Bois
A Short Parochial and Commercial History of Jersey
    – Philip Ahier
The War in the Channel Islands – Winston Ramsay
The Harbour that Failed — William Davies

*Those books which are no longer generally available through
booksellers may be studied at the Central Library, Royal Square,
St. Helier.*

ACKNOWLEDGEMENTS

The author's very special thanks go to local historian
Joan Stevens and Jersey's Conservation Officer, Dr.
Mike Romeril for the encouragement, expertise and
time they gave during the preparation of this book.
To Jean Le Boutillier for the preparation of the
maps, and to Richard Mayne and Gerald Amy for the
loan of historic photographs of the Island. The
author's gratitude is also extended to those whose
specialised knowledge was given constantly,
willingly and with great patience:

Margaret Finlaison, Jersey Heritage Trust;
Michael Ginns, Channel Islands Occupation
Society;
Stanley Clowsley, National Trust for Jersey;
Dr. Arthur Mourant, La Société Jersiaise;
Graeme Journeaux, Department of Public Building
and Works;
Mike Stentiford, Royal Society for the Protection
of Birds.

Many more people gave advice and information,
including parish officials, the compilers of parish
Treasuries and authorities on specific places.
Thanks go to all of them and to everybody who, in a
variety of ways, helped the author to "Explore
Jersey".

FOREWORD

by his Excellency General Sir Peter
Whiteley, GCB, OBE,
Lieutenant-Governor of Jersey
1979 - 1984

Many authoritative books are available to the student of Channel Island history. There are likewise definitive works on flora and fauna, geology, archaeology, traditions and way of life. Tourist guides are available for consultation on places of entertainment, leisure and recreation, beauty spots and scenic walks and rides.

Beth Lloyd has produced a book which at last fulfils a long felt need for a work which brings all these aspects of our island life together in a handy and eminently readable volume. Here we have an invaluable illustrated guide for the island's many annual visitors, while to those who live in Jersey it will provide a most interesting and useful companion on an island walkabout, parish by parish, and a catalyst to further study in depth of a multitude of fascinating aspects of the Jersey scene.

Peter Whiteley

CONTENTS

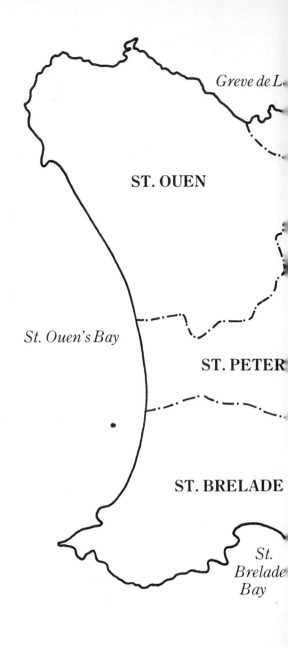

Introduction	6
ST. HELIER	**12**
Vallée des Vaux	15
Royal Square	16
Old Town and Parade	18
Westmount and People's Park	21
Markets	22
Fort Regent	23
Pier Road Museum	24
Harbour	25
Elizabeth Castle	26
First Tower	28
ST. LAWRENCE	**29**
Coronation Park – Millbrook	30
Waterworks Valley (walk)	31
Le Rât Cottage – Morel Farm (walk)	32
German Military Underground Hospital	35
ST. BRELADE	**36**
Railway Walk	37
St. Aubin	40
St. Brelade's Bay	42
Noirmont and Portelet	44
La Corbière	47
ST. PETER	**48**
Val de la Mare Reservoir walk	49
St. Peter's Valley – Le Moulin de Quétivel	50
Motor Museum – St. Peter's Bunker	52
Sunset Nurseries	54
ST. OUEN'S BAY	**55**
Beach	56
Les Blanches Banques	57
La Mare au Seigneur (St. Ouen's Pond)	58
Defences and Fortifications	59
Le Mielle de Morville	60
ST. OUEN	**61**
Dolmen des Monts, Grantez	62
Les Landes	63
St. Ouen's Manor	64
Le Pinacle	67
L'Etacq Woodcrafts	68
Battle of Flowers Museum	69
ST. MARY	**71**
Grève de Lecq Barracks	72
La Mare Vineyards	73
Jersey Butterfly Centre	74
ST. JOHN	**75**
Bonne Nuit	76
Heatherbrae Farm	77
TRINITY	**79**
Les Platons and La Belle Hougue (inc. climb to cave)	80
Bouley Bay	82
Jersey Wildlife Preservation Trust	84
ST. MARTIN	**87**
Rozel (including walk to mill)	89
Perquage Path (through Rozel Woods)	90
St. Catherine's Bay	91
Mont Orgueil Castle	92
Le Couperon Dolmen and Saie Harbour + La Pouquelaye de Faldouet	95
Victoria Tower + Geoffrey's Leap	97
Gorey Pier	99

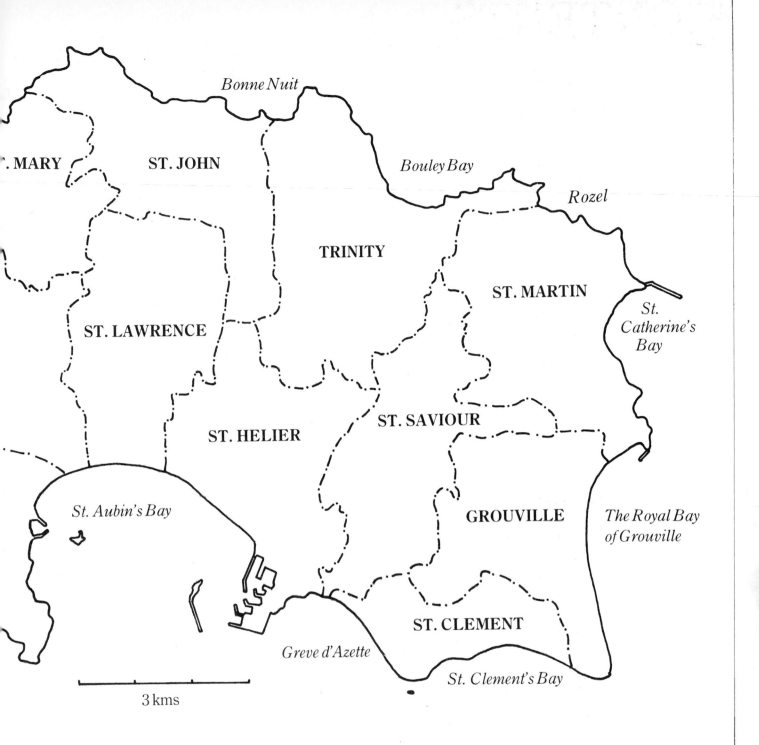

3 kms

GROUVILLE	100
Grouville Bay	101
Grouville Common (and Marsh)	102
Jersey Pottery	103
La Rocque	105
La Hougue Bie	106
ST. CLEMENT	108
Green Island	109
Samarès Manor	110
ST. SAVIOUR	113
Howard Davis Park	114
Longueville Manor Colombier	116
COASTAL WALKS	117

The 'Price Guide' given for each attraction is simply a guide to the cost of entry.

Cost for a family, 2 adults and 2 children at time of publication

A. – Over £5
B. – £3 - £5
C. – £2 - £3
D. – Under £2
E. – Under £1

Prices may change in the future but the guides should remain a useful pointer to which are relatively dear and which are relatively cheap. As the most expensive sites offer a complete day out with special attractions, the classification is no indication of value for money.

The maps in this book are intended only as a rough guide. For more detailed information the 1:25000 O.S. map of Jersey is recommended.

INTRODUCTION

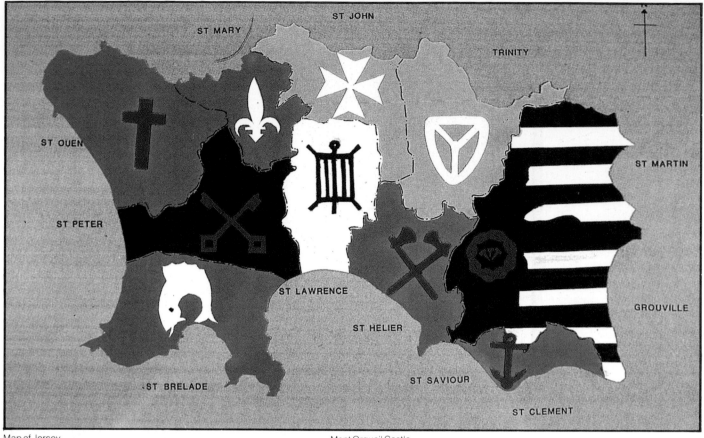

Map of Jersey

Mont Orgueil Castle

Jersey is the most southerly of the British Isles. It slopes to the south and is approximately ten miles by five. For its size it would be hard to equal its variety of scenery, its wealth of history and its sheer beauty.

It could be thought that an area of forty-five square miles with a permanent population of something over 76,000 would have little, other than buildings, to explore. But approach the Island by air and you see the lush valleys, the well-kept fields and the unspoilt coast-line. Arrive by sea and the rocky grandeur of La Corbière, the sweep of St. Aubin's Bay and picturesque Elizabeth Castle are your introduction to the Island. The coast-line itself offers infinite variety – majestic cliffs, exposed bays, sandy beaches and rocky coves.

Unlike the neighbouring islands of Guernsey and Alderney, which have some of the oldest rocks in the British Isles, Jersey's are the late Pre-cambrian or Brioverian shales, laid down as mud on the sea floor some seven hundred to nine hundred million years ago. Towards the end of that period volcanic rocks were poured out over these shales and some one to two hundred million years later, during the great Cadomian mountain-building period, granite "magma" (deep seated molten rock) was injected.

These shales, volcanics and granites account for about ninety per cent of the area and granite of varying shades of pink forms about a third of the Island and has been used extensively for building purposes over the centuries. The Conglomerate or "pudding-stone" of the Rozel area was laid down later – perhaps four hundred million years ago, when great torrents eroded the mountains. This consolidated coarse mixture of pebbles and boulders has also been quarried and used to build such structures as St. Catherine's Breakwater.

Grosnez Castle

Around two hundred and fifty thousand years ago, when Jersey was a rocky plateau lying in a low plain, Palaeolithic men followed herds of animals across Europe. Remains of these men and their prey have been found in a well-preserved shelter at La Cotte de St. Brelade, but for reasons of safety and preservation, this area is closed to the public. For those interested in archaeology though, there is still plenty to see. Centuries of land cultivation have caused the loss of many settlements, but there are still numerous monuments of prehistory.

Victor Hugo's famous quote that the Channel Islands are small portions of France which have fallen into the sea and have been swept up by England is, in the very broadest sense, true. Jersey was part of the Duchy of Normandy at the time of the Conquest, and the language and many of the laws and customs of the Island are inherited from those early years. When King John lost Normandy, Jersey remained loyal to the English crown – a loyalty that has been unswerving over the centuries, notwithstanding the constant threat of invasion. The Island's castles and forts are proof of that threat, as are the 18th century round towers and the Martello towers built during the Napoleonic wars. Other fortifications have now become part of the landscape: stark reminders of a tragic period in Jersey's modern history – the German occupation during World War II.

St. Helier Harbour

Dolmen De Faldouet

German troops parading through St. Helier 3rd July 1943 (R. Mayne)

St. Peter's Mill

St. Mary's church

Jersey cows

The government of the Island used to be in the hands of the Jurats – twelve elected magistrates who also tried criminals and settled disputes, in what came to be called the Royal Court. Nowadays the Jurats act solely as judges and a democratic parliament known as the States formulates Jersey's internal legislation. This is composed of twelve Senators (elected on an Island-wide basis), the parish Constables and twenty-eight parish Deputies. The Bailiff, who is appointed by the Crown, presides over the States and the Royal Court. The Lieutenant-Governor (the Queen's representative), the Dean, the Attorney-General and the Solicitor-General are also appointed by the Crown. They sit in the States and are entitled to speak, but have no vote.

Eight of the twelve parish churches existed before 1066 and all are rich in history. Even after the separation from Normandy, for political as well as religious reasons, Jersey remained part of the diocese of Coutances. After the Reformation the Island became staunchly Calvinist and most of the rectors were French Protestants and it was not until the reign of James I that Anglicanism became the accepted religion. During the 18th century the Methodist movement, which started among the troops, spread rapidly. Aided by a visit from John Wesley the religion gained many converts and there are now many Methodist chapels in the Island. With the influx of French royalist refugees, Roman Catholicism returned to Jersey, though on sufferance, and was reinforced with the immigration of many French and Irish labourers.

Les Routeurs, St. Saviour

Over the centuries there have been as many as forty-seven watermills situated on the fourteen Island streams. Few survive today, but one – Le Moulin de Quétivel, has been restored as a working mill by the National Trust for Jersey. There were also a number of windmills of which four still survive – albeit without their sails (although St. Peter's Mill – now a public house – has a non-functional set). These mills belonged to the Crown or the Lord of the Manor (Seigneur) and were of vital importance both to the farmers for grinding their corn and to the owners as a source of revenue.

Jersey is divided into twelve parishes and each parish into vingtaines. The head of each parish is the Constable who also heads the parish honorary police, assisted by centeniers, vingteniers and constable's officers. One of their responsibilities is the bi-annual branchage inspection. The roads of each parish are inspected to ensure that land-owners have cut their roadside banks and that trees and hedges are trimmed to a stipulated height to allow the free passage of farm vehicles and other forms of transport.

Branchage in St. Mary

Parish boundary stones can be discovered by the pedestrian. These date back to the time when each vingtaine was responsible for repairing its own roads. Milestones bearing a letter and a number can also be seen on the old military roads. All mileage is taken from the statue of George II in the Royal Square and the stones show the initial of the Parish and the number of miles from the statue.

Colombiers – or dovecots – used to be the sole prerogative of the Seigneurs (Lords of the Manor), but later the privilege was extended and there remain eleven of these buildings.

Lavoirs – used for the household wash in time past, and abreuvoirs – drinking troughs for animals, can also be discovered along country lanes.

Look out for marriage stones – usually forming a lintel over the front door of a house. They bear a date and the syllabic initials of a couple with one or perhaps two interlocking hearts in the middle. The stones may commemorate a marriage, the building of the house or an important family event. Witches' stones can also be seen on many old granite chimneys. These flat stones, emerging horizontally from the stacks, certainly look like resting places for tired witches but the mundane reason for their existence is that they were designed to stop rain water seeping under a thatched roof. Why, though, are there so many to be found on houses that never had a thatch?

One of Jersey's main industries is agriculture and even the steepest côtil is cultivated. Of course the Jersey cow is famous throughout the world and cattle shows are held during the late spring and early summer. You do not have to be a farmer to soak up the sun and the atmosphere at one of these events.

Parade Gardens in early May

Jersey Orchid

Brent Goose (Stentiford)

Wild garlic

Throughout the year the Island is ablaze with colour from both wild and cultivated varieties of flowers and shrubs. Camellias and magnolias are common-place in spring-time gardens, while wild daffodils (lent lilies) and primroses are scattered over the common land. The headlands' yellow blanket of gorse changes to a purple carpet of thrift and heather as the year progresses, while in the hedgerows flowering garlic runs riot, often hiding the shrinking violet. Hydrangeas are almost wild in Jersey, and of course there is the Jersey lily (*Amaryllis belladonna*) which can be seen in the front garden of almost every farmhouse. For those who enjoy other people's gardens, the Jersey Association of Youth and Friendship has an Open Garden scheme which runs every summer and includes many types of garden.

Central Market

Flocks of Brent geese winter in Jersey after breeding in the Arctic. This is just one species of bird that can be seen on Jersey's shoreline, which also offers the usual rock-pool delights of numerous species of molluscs and crustaceans. One mollusc indigenous to Jersey is the ormer (oreille de mer). Traditionally caught at very low tide, the ormer is a Jersey delicacy. Unfortunately, with the advent of skin-diving, their population has declined sharply and it is now illegal to gather ormers by diving.

For those who prefer to do their exploring in a sedentary position there are two alternatives both of which are constant reminders of Jersey's independence and heritage. Jersey's own coinage began in 1813 when the Royal Mint struck silver tokens with face values of three shillings and eighteen pence to replace the French coins which had ceased with the onset of the Napoleonic Wars – since then Jersey has had its own coinage.

In 1969 Jersey established its own independent Postal Administration and ever since, Jersey stamps have become collectors' items. The Administration ensures that these all bear in some way on the history of Jersey and its people – whether in their home Island or playing their part in the world at large. As the years pass, a collection of the Island's stamps becomes more and more an illustrated guide to Jersey – past and present.

Exploring Jersey is fun . . . and safe as long as the simple rules of common-sense are followed. Cliffs can be dangerous, so keep to the paths unless you are an expert and properly equipped – and always watch the state of the tide when exploring caves, rocks and gullies.

Metal detecting is banned on all lands belonging to the States, the Société Jersiaise and the National Trust.

Please preserve our heritage and enjoy the beautiful Island of Jersey.

THE COUNTRY CODE

Guard against all risks of fire
Fasten all gates
Keep dogs under proper control
Keep to the paths across farm land
Avoid damaging fences, hedges and walls
Leave no litter – take it home
Safeguard water supplies
Protect wildlife, wild plants and trees
Go carefully along country roads
Respect the life of the countryside

ST. HELIER

The parish of St. Helier includes the town of the same name, which is the administrative capital and main shopping centre. Over a third of the island's population live in the parish, although several rural areas come within its six vingtaines. The town can be confusing to the visitor, and parking is difficult, although there are a number of multi-storey parks which are clearly signed. For the convenience of the pedestrian, old-fashioned sign-posts have recently been erected in the centre of town.

The pedestrian precincts make shopping pleasurable, and for the visitor the lack of V.A.T. gives an added bonus to exploring the town shops.

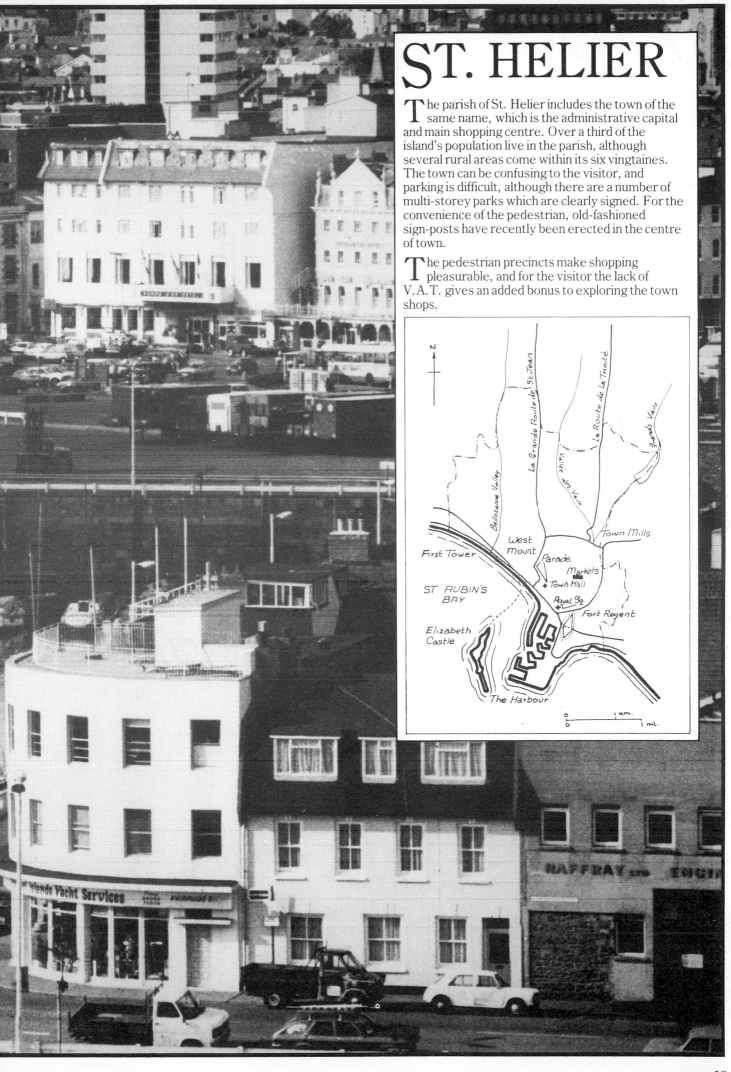

AUGRES HOUSE — SOLD

LA HURETTE — SOLD

LA GRAND MAISON — SOLD

*Of the few first class luxury houses
which were offered for sale in Jersey during the year,
Beck & Deane successfully negotiated the sale
of the properties illustrated.*

RESIDENTIAL INVESTMENT and COMMERCIAL PROPERTY

Beck & Deane

1 Waterloo Street, St. Helier, Jersey, C.I. Telephone 0534-72356
Red Houses, St. Brelade, Jersey, C.I. Telephone 0534-45586
SURVEYORS : ESTATE AGENTS : VALUERS

VALLÉE DES VAUX

Bus route 4
to bottom of
Trinity Hill

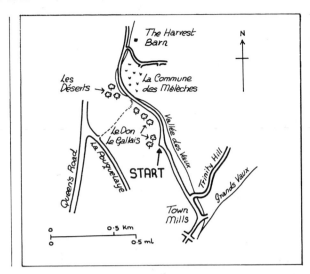

Stream to the Water
Garden

The Water Garden

Town Mills at the foot of Vallée des Vaux and Grands Vaux, is the site of the old water-mills which used to serve the town area.

Vallée des Vaux, or the Valley of Small Vales, is often called "the lung of St. Helier" and with good reason, for although within easy reach of the centre of town, it is green and peaceful in all seasons. For the really energetic it is possible to walk from the junction at Trinity Hill, right up the valley into Trinity and so on to Bonne Nuit Bay without using major roads or passing any built-up areas. The following describes a smaller area for those with less time and energy.

Coming from town, turn left into the valley at the foot of Trinity Hill. After about a quarter of a mile an S-bend is reached, and for car drivers this is a good place to park. On the right-hand-side, over a granite wall, can be seen a meadow which used to be the mill pond. On the left-hand-side is a wooded area. This was the first property to be given to the National Trust for Jersey and is called Le Don Le Gallais (Don meaning 'gift of'). There are some European hornbeam (*calpinus betulus*) trees here which are thought to be comparatively rare. Two houses and some private land mean that one cannot take an uninterrupted walk through Le Don Le Gallais, but once past these, the woodland walks are undisturbed until the steps leading up to La Pouquelaye and Queen's Road are reached. Some people may wish to start their walk from these steps which are found at the foot of High View Lane, La Pouquelaye.

On the other side of the road, opposite the second, bigger area of Le Don Le Gallais, is a water garden belonging to the parish. It has two bridges over the brook. The sounds of running water and bird-song, together with the profusion of plants and trees, make this a good resting place.

About fifty yards past La Pouquelaye steps is another National Trust property, Les Déserts. This is reached by stepping stones over the brook and has been made into an arboretum with trees such as southern beech, cherry, oak and nothofagus. A cedar has been planted above a plaque to Brigadier Anderton, President of the National Trust for Jersey 1962-1971.

On the other side of the road is a slope of common land known as La Commune des Mélèches. This is gorse-covered and can get overgrown, so it is advisable to wear adequate walking shoes, but the view of the valley from the top is well worth the effort. There are two entrances to this common – one is a little way past La Pouquelaye Steps and the other is found by taking the next road to the right, before the Harvest Barn and turning right again down a track.

ST HELIER ROYAL SQUARE

This pleasant square with its spreading chestnut trees is a good place to start an exploration of St. Helier. From time immemorial it was the centre of Island life as until the 19th century it was the market (La Place du Marché). Not only was produce sold there but proclamations and laws were read from the market cross, witches were burned and criminals were whipped, caged and pilloried. However, in 1800 it was decided to move the market as it caused too much noise and commotion to be situated outside the Royal Court and States Chamber.

The present buildings housing our seat of government are worth visiting. The States sit most Tuesdays and from the public gallery, entered from Halkett Place, can be seen the second oldest Royal Mace in the world, given to the Island by Charles II and inscribed "Not all doth he deem worthy of such a reward". The Royal Court has a fine collection of paintings, including a copy of John Singleton Copley's famous painting of the death of Major Peirson by W. Holyoake. The States were out-bidden for the original which hangs in the Tate Gallery.

The Chamber of Commerce building to the east of the square is of interest because the Jersey Chamber of Commerce is the oldest in the English speaking world. It was founded in 1768 by a group of merchants who wanted to protect their trading interests.

Granite Memorial to Baron de Rullecourt outside the west door of the town church.

Royal Square.

The statue of George II is probably the finest piece of statuary in the Island. Made by John Cheere in 1751, it stands on or near the site of the market cross which was destroyed during the Reformation. In gilded lead, it depicts the King dressed as a Roman emperor. It was unveiled at a grand ceremony in the presence of the Governor and Bailiff.

The Battle of Jersey took place here in 1781. An expedition of French soldiers led by Charles Félix Macquart, Baron de Rullecourt, had landed at La Rocque (see Grouville) and had marched into town. The Lieutenant-Governor, Major Moses Corbet, was surprised at his home and had surrendered, but Major Francis Peirson led the 95th and 78th Regiments into battle, and assisted by the Militia, defeated the French in less than ten minutes. Both de Rullecourt and Peirson were killed in or near the Peirson Public House where red discs apparently mark bullet holes made during the battle.

Towards the end of 1944 a stone-mason called Le Guyader was given the job of relaying and levelling the flag-stones in the square. As he worked he changed the position of certain stones to make a V for victory, keeping the finished product covered with sand until the work was completed, by which time the war was over. After the war the initials EGA (making VEGA) and the date 1945 were added to commemorate the arrival of the Swedish ship Vega which had brought much needed Red cross supplies in December 1944.

The corn market used to be situated at the western end of Royal Square. The ground floor of this building is now a bank, and the original granite arches of the market have been preserved in the banking hall. On the first floor of the same building, in what is now the United Club, there used to be an assembly hall. John Wesley is known to have preached there in 1787.

The Old Market in the eighteenth century – an artist's impression.

The Parish Church of St. Helier

Opposite this building is the military picket house of 1803. The porch, resting on four slim cast-iron columns, was added in 1835. The drain heads are inscribed Geo III and bear the royal cypher. Read the sundial on the south wall, which was renovated in 1965.

To visit the church one must cross Church Street. A simple enough procedure these days, with the only hazard being the traffic coming from the left. Not so in days gone by: there used to be a brook running down the centre of the road, so ladies had to tuck up their petticoats to get across. Hence the old name La Rue Trousse Cotillon.

St. Helier's Church is dedicated to Jersey's patron saint St. Helier who was murdered in 555, and who is commemorated by a statue above the north door. The original church was probably built in the 10th or 11th century: it certainly existed in 1066.

During the Civil War in 1643 when the town was held by the Parliamentarians and Sir Philippe de Carteret was defending Elizabeth Castle, the church was hit several times by cannon fired from the castle. The diarist Jean Chevalier commented that this was probably due to bad marksmanship rather than Sir Philippe's wishes!

Charles, later King Charles II, attended a service in the church in April 1646. He was then only fifteen but "His chair was placed in front of the pulpit with carpets on either side. A small table was set before him with a cushion for his elbow when he knelt. Sweet-scented herbs were scattered round, and the table was strewn with roses."

During the rule of the Parliamentarians the church lost many of its possessions, including the font which was found on a farm being used as a pig trough.

Major Peirson is buried near the chancel steps under a stone simply inscribed "Peirson", and in the churchyard, immediately opposite the west door, a small granite memorial stone reads "Rullecourt 6 janvier 1781".

There is a gateway into Bond Street to the west of the church. In this opening, towards Broad Street, can be seen an iron screen which was originally in the chapel of the old prison in Newgate Street.

Bond Street used to be called La Rue de la Madelaine because on its east side, adjoining the churchyard there once stood a chapel of that name, which was used as a poor-house after the Reformation.

Statue of St. Helier

OLD TOWN AND PARADE

From the church, walk down Library Place which takes its name from the building at No. 5. Philip Falle (1656-1742) wrote the first history of Jersey and gave a large number of books to the Island, making this house one of the oldest public libraries in the British Isles. The house was built in 1736-41 and the drain-heads still bear the initials PF and the date 1736.

Le Sueur Obelisk in Broad Street

The Parade looking west

La Croix de la Reine

From Library Place enter Broad Street, originally called La Grande Rue as it was the main thoroughfare of the town. Immediately facing is an obelisk to the memory of Pierre Le Sueur (1811-53) who was five times Constable of St. Helier. This memorial, which stands on a tall plinth decorated with traditional lamps and lion-head water fountains, was erected the year after his death. Walk down Broad Street, perhaps visiting the Post Office and Philatelic Bureau housed in an Edwardian building on your left, until you reach Charing Cross. This marks the western boundary of the old town and a public water supply, La Pompe de Bas (the eastern boundary being La Pompe du Haut at Snow Hill). At Charing Cross stands La Croix de La Reine, a carved granite cross with panels cut in relief depicting the symbols of the parish. It was here that in 1978 Her Majesty the Queen was presented with a book about the Cross from the parish of St. Helier.

In 1693 a prison in the form of a gate-house was built at Charing Cross. Prior to that date prisoners had been kept at Mont Orgueil Castle, which was inconvenient for all concerned as they had to be brought into town for trial. In 1806 General Sir George Don became Lieutenant-Governor. He disliked the narrow arch so much that he decided to move the prison to Newgate Street. The gate-house prison was demolished in 1811 and, because the Newgate Street prison was not completed until 1814, for three years serious criminals were kept in Elizabeth Castle and petty criminals at the hospital which was a poor house at that time.

The Town Hall in York Street was built in 1872 by Le Sueur and Bree. The interior has been attractively modernized and in the Assembly Room, which can be visited when no meeting is taking place, is a display of the Parish silver and pictures by well-known Jersey artists. The Committee Room, which can be visited by arrangement, has a fine display of water colours by J. Le Capelain and "La Repasseuse", an extremely valuable painting by J.L. David. A free pamphlet "A Tour of St. Helier" can be obtained from the Town Hall.

There are small tar swastikas on the front walls of the Town Hall, about four feet from the pavement. These were put there in 1944 by men from a brigade of German army engineers who, when they arrived in Jersey, were so appalled to see swastikas painted on the homes of collaborators, that they decided to daub other buildings in similar fashion.

Old Street, to your left, has been extensively redeveloped. It was here that several years ago, unmistakable evidence of a 13th century house was found. This was surprising to historians who had always supposed that area to have been uninhabitable marsh-land and sandy wastes. In fact the Parade was called Les Mielles until general Don enclosed it and made it a parade-ground. An Artillery Brigade was housed along the northern side, hence Cannon Street. The monument to General Don by Pierre Robinet was put up in 1886. It depicts the General standing between figures of Commerce and Industry and flanked by cannon.

The Town Hall
Statue of General Don

The Parade looking east

All Saints Church

All Saints Church was built in 1835 on the site of the Strangers' Cemetery. By 1832 this burial ground was full and its ground level some eight feet higher than the surrounding area. When the church was built the ground was scarped, but even so the building is perched on a four-foot elevation.

The Hospital, which borders the south of the Parade, was built in the late eighteenth century as a work-house. The army took it over as a barracks in 1779 and in 1783 it was partially destroyed by an explosion of gun-powder. It was burnt again in 1859 and the present building, which is now being extended and modernized, was erected in 1861.

The gardens in the Parade are a delight to the eye and it is a popular place for relaxation during the working day.

If you walk a little further into Cheapside and turn right down Elizabeth Lane, a few yards on the left can be seen what is thought to be the oldest existing house in St. Helier. It is the rear part of a private house now called Glen Rest and was built in the early 17th century. It is hard to imagine now what an isolated house it must have been, built on desolate sand-dunes and very close to the sea.

WESTMOUNT AND PEOPLE'S PARK

To the west of Cheapside is People's Park, a large recreation area which includes a children's playground. Above the park are the tree-covered slopes of Westmount, which can also be entered from the top of Westmount Road or from St. Aubin's Road beyond the Inn on the Park. Dominating this area is what used to be called Mont Patibulaire, or

Gallows Hill, as it was here that public executions took place, the last one being recorded in 1829. The gallows consisted of four permanent pillars, and before each hanging the necessary cross-beams were added. One such execution was carried out in 1555 on a priest called Richard Averty who "grievously oppressed the poor folk who were faithful to the Reformed Church". When his maid-servant gave birth to a baby boy he baptised it, then strangled it and buried it under the hearth of his house: a crime so unpopular that it helped stop any counter-Reformation in Jersey. He was sentenced to be "dragged to the gallows and hanged till he was dead, his body to be left on the gibbet till it should rot away".

The gallows probably stood on flat land at the top of the hill as several bodies in uniform were unearthed in the area when Westmount House was built.

Lower down and across Westmount Road, is a plaque marking the spot where Major Peirson prepared for the Battle of Jersey. The Highlanders, who were billeted in the Hospital, had withdrawn to the area and were eventually joined by the Militia and the 95th Foot under the command of the 24-year-old Major Peirson, because his senior officers were on Christmas leave. The Militia Colonels placed themselves under the orders of the young Major who, as we have seen, successfully led the 1,600 men into the attack on the French in Royal Square.

Below this hill there used to be an inlet called Horse-shoe Quarry where the parish refuse was dumped. This has long since been covered and these days a highly efficient incinerator in Bellozanne Valley copes with all the island's refuse.

The gazebo with the peaked roof above the Inn on the Park is not what it seems: it was built by the Germans in July 1942 as a machine-gun post.

From the slopes of Westmount it is easy to see why Victoria Gardens was known as Triangle Park until the statue of Queen Victoria was moved there in 1976. The statue, by Georges Wallet, was "erigé par le peuple" in the Weighbridge Gardens, now the bus depôt, to mark the Jubilee of 1887. It is made of bronze cast in Paris, and stands on a plinth of La Moye granite designed by Adolphus Curry.

A little way past the St. Aubin's Road entrance to Westmount is the Animal Cemetery, opened in 1928. This acre or so of land contains the graves of many cats and dogs as well as a golden goat and a "wonderful horse". Animals with names like Prince, Snaffles and Snookey have memorials ranging from "only a cat but almost human" to

"Here rest the relics of our friends below, Blest with more sense than half the folk we know."

Animal Cemetery

Statue of Queen Victoria

People's Park

THE MARKETS

Closed Sundays, Thursday afternoons, and Bank Holidays.

Central Market

The Central Market, between Beresford Street and Halkett Place is the busiest retail trading premises in the Channel Islands. Greengrocers and butchers predominate but the thirty-four tenants sell a wide variety of basic and non-basic goods. There has been a market on this site since 1804 when market trading moved from the Royal Square.

The fountain in Central Market

The States had purchased the plot of marshy ground from a Mr Le Maistre in 1796 and from the proceeds of seven lotteries they built an open market closely modelled on the market in the city of Bath. From John Stead's 'Picture of Jersey' written in 1809 we learn that "it forms an extensive oblong, the front is an elegant entrance of three gates, four massy stone columns with an iron palisade running the whole length of the area . . . the whole paved with Swanage stone . . . order and cleanliness prevail throughout . . . the piazza accommodates vendors of vegetables, fruit, flowers and poultry whilst in the centre there are four rows of butchers' stalls". There was a total of forty stalls and St. Helier market was described by Thomas Lyle as . . . "One of the finest in Europe". A model of this market can be seen at the Jersey Museum in Pier Road.

In 1881 it was decided to build a new market to celebrate the centenary of the Battle of Jersey and on 9th September 1882 the present building, designed by T. W. Helliwell, was opened. Granite outside walls and thirty-seven pillars support the roof and dome, which originally contained eighty tons of glass. This glass has recently been replaced by opaque p.v.c. sheeting, one-fifth the weight of the glass which, while letting in light, eliminates rays harmful to fresh produce. The centrepiece was, and still is, a fifteen-foot high four-tier ornamental fountain surrounded by a gold-fish pond. Two iron gates from the original market were retained at the entrances from Market Street and Hilgrove Lane. These incorporate designs of bunches of grapes, a peacock and the heads of various animals and birds.

During the German occupation of World War II the market was open four hours a day. Only local produce was on offer and stall-holders were entitled to refuse to serve the occupying forces. Even so supplies were short. Swedes predominated and long queues formed when other delicacies such as rhubarb became available. As can be seen, there is no such shortage today!

Just across Beresford Street is Beresford Market, sometimes called the Old Market or more generally the Fish Market. The fish market moved here in 1841 and there was also a French Market in the area which later became known as the Foreign Market. In the late 1800's a Toy Market was also established off Beresford Street.

Alterations and restorations were made in 1873 and 1936, and Beresford Market was completely renovated in 1972.

The cattle market, built in Minden Place in 1841, is now a multi-storey car park.

FORT REGENT ENTERTAINMENT AND SPORTS CENTRE

Price Code A
Admission charges, which allow free enjoyment of all facilities except sport, vary according to time and day. For details ask at reception or telephone 73000.
Open daily 9am-11pm for sports. 10am-10pm high season and 10am-6pm low season for exhibitions, museums, and entertainment.
Yearly and winter membership available
Cable cars from Snow Hill (high season)
Lift and escalator from Pier Road car park
Suitable for disabled
Restaurant and cafe.

Currently attracting around one million visitors a year, this entertainment and sports centre is Jersey's most popular tourist attraction.

Built between 1806 and 1814 to defend the town during the Napoleonic Wars, Fort Regent was continuously garrisoned by units of the British Army until the 1930s, although ironically the only shots ever fired in anger from it were by German anti-aircraft guns against Allied planes during World War Two.

On March 1st 1958 the States of Jersey purchased the Fort from the British Government, but it was not until December 1967 that proposals to develop the twenty-three acre site into a leisure centre were finally approved. Now there is a wide variety of sports, recreations and entertainment within the complex as well as shops, cafes, restaurants, bars and a discothèque.

Throughout the day during the summer the indoor Piazza stage comes to life with entertainment for all the family, and surrounding the Piazza, set in what was once the original barracks, there are exhibitions, museums and an aquarium.

To the south are the two indoor heated swimming pools complete with solarium, spectator gallery and sun terrace. Outside the pool complex one enters the world of the fairground with free rides for all on the big wheel, carousel, astroglide, dodgems and swinging gyms, while further along the children can enjoy the giant snake slide, the giant elephant slide and the American log-style playground while others may prefer a game of mini-golf.

For those who prefer something more peaceful, there are the aviaries and rose gardens to stroll through, and the grassy slopes of the outer ramparts offer marvellous views of St. Helier.

Sporting enthusiasts are well catered for, with badminton, squash, table-tennis, snooker and darts on offer.

The Gloucester Hall, opened by the Duke of Gloucester on 23rd September 1978, can be transformed from a sports arena into a 2,000 seat auditorium in a matter of hours. Here great entertainers such as Cannon and Ball, Sir Harry Secombe, Dave Allen, Jim Davidson and The Nolans have appeared during the high season. Similar acts are brought over each year.

Originally Fort Regent was designed to be impregnable and to keep people out. Now its role is reversed and within its great walls there is surely something for everyone to enjoy.

JERSEY MUSEUM, PIER ROAD

Victorian Room

The Société Jersiaise is a voluntary organisation founded in 1873 for the study and conservation of Jersey's natural and cultural heritage. Over the years it has grown in membership and influence, and this museum has become one of its most important assets. The building also acts as the Société's headquarters and houses its well-stocked library.

The house itself was donated to the Société in 1893 by Jurat J. G. Falle, one of its founder members, and the museum has remained here ever since. It is spread over four floors, and its uncluttered lay-out is a credit to the Société Jersiaise.

Apple Crusher

The house as it stands was built in 1817 by one Philippe Nicolle to back on to his ship-building yard. On this lower-ground level is a marine biological room and what could be described as a "law and order" room which includes a large treadmill which, in the last century, was manned by up to twelve prisoners at a time to operate a pepper mill.

The Lillie Langtry Room is proving very popular. Here hangs her famous portrait by Sir Edward Poynter, and letters and posters from her acting career are on show together with dresses from the television series based on the life of this famous Jersey woman.

It is natural that Jersey's history has always been inextricably tied to the sea, and on the first floor can be found the Maritime Room. Next door is a reconstruction of a chemist's shop circa 1880 and on the floor above are two delightful Victorian rooms, depicting a time of great prosperity in Jersey.

There is plenty more to see: permanent displays of silver, natural history, postage, coins, medals and bank-notes as well as a photographic collection.

Over the years literally thousands of items have been donated and with the space available it was simply not possible to exhibit them all. Now an extension is being built where, on the top floor will be a new Island Art Gallery which will house the permanent collection from the Barreau Art Gallery and the Le Maistre Bequest. On the middle floor it is planned to tell the story of the Island from prehistoric times up to the present day, and on the ground floor there will be a temporary exhibition gallery, an audio-visual presentation and some special permanent exhibitions.

One priceless document owned by the Société is the proclamation of Charles II signed in 1649, eleven years before he was proclaimed King anywhere else in the British Isles. Soon, this and other historical documents will be on permanent display.

1880 Chemist Shop

Price Code C
Entrance from Pier Road or Weighbridge (Summer only)
Open all year
Monday-Saturday 10-5
Guide Book

Pier Road entrance

SOCIETE JERSIAISE

Harbour

The Port of St. Helier has changed considerably in the last few years and indeed is still developing. In 1981 it was decided to reclaim some thirty-five acres to the west of the Albert Pier, and the walls are now completed, so it is possible to walk along these walls from the Esplanade to the Albert Pier which has its own raised walk-way from its head to the Weighbridge.

Looking at the harbour today, it is hard to imagine that its development only began in the eighteenth century. Before, there was just one small jetty near La Folie Inn. Even after the addition of the North and South piers and the Merchant's Wharf, the harbour was totally inadequate: it was tidal and offered little shelter and many merchants still preferred to use St. Aubin's Harbour. When the Duke of Gloucester paid a State Visit to Jersey in 1817 he had to scramble on all fours over seaweed-covered rocks to reach the beach where the States and Militia were lined up to greet him – not the most dignified start to a Royal visit!

In those times the fishing industry was booming and apparently the harbour became increasingly congested, so it was decided to create an outer harbour. Between 1841 and 1846 the Victoria Pier was built, which was followed by the construction of the Albert Pier between 1847 and 1853.

For the rest of the century the authorities struggled with the problems posed by the unnatural harbour and the ever-increasing passenger flow. Two breakwaters were planned but were never fully completed because the southern one was destroyed during a gale. Dredging was undertaken to allow passenger vessels to berth at most states of the tide and the North Pier was widened to form the New North Quay.

Some small improvements were made earlier this century, but it was not until the 1970s, by which time the harbour had become totally inadequate, that any major development took place. In 1975 a new plan came into being – the results of which can now be seen. The piers have been widened and strengthened and to counter the lack of natural deep water, the area between New North Quay and Albert Pier has been dredged to allow ships entry at most times. But perhaps the most exciting development is the new yacht marina. For years there had been a long waiting list for marina facilities, and visiting yachtsmen had to be discouraged from visiting the island as there was simply nowhere for them to berth. The proposition for a new marina was approved by the States in June 1977 and it opened in September 1981. 250 visiting yachts can now be accommodated and there are 180 permanent berths. A chandlery shop has been opened and all the usual marina facilities are available. Everyone benefits by its presence and it adds a picturesque touch to a gentle stroll round the harbour. Fishing off the harbour walls is a popular pastime, and at certain times of the year vessels can be chartered for deep-sea fishing.

Victoria Pier and Elizabeth Castle from Mount Bingham

ELIZABETH CASTLE AND THE HERMITAGE

Price Code B
Open 9.30-6.
Tea Room
Guide Book
D.U.K.Ws return fare –
Price Code B

Much of the Island's history and legend is concentrated on the small island of L'Islet which, being three quarters of a mile out to sea, is cut off by the rising tide. Nowadays there are commercial "D.U.K.W.'s" which regularly ferry visitors either by sea or along the shingle causeway, but at low tide the walk is both pleasant and invigorating.

Legend has it that St. Helier, the 6th century patron saint of the Island, lived in a cave on a rock close by L'Islet. Many stories have grown up around this saint's life, but the tale most widely known is that he was axed to death by Saxon pirates in the year 555. Some say that the sea then carried his body to Bréville, a village in Normandy where he had wished to be buried. This is not impossible, and there is indeed a church there dedicated to him. Each year, on or around St. Helier's Day (16th July) a pilgrimage is made to the 12th century oratory built over his cave and a wreath is laid to his memory.

In the 12th century William FitzHamon, a knight and friend of Henry II built an Abbey on L'Islet which for thirty years was both rich and prestigious, but when the king's mother, Matilda, founded another Augustinian Abbey in Cherbourg a great rivalry ensued which culminated in St. Helier being reduced to a priory. It never fully regained its former glory and over the centuries became more and more run down until it ceased to exist at the time of the Reformation.

The Lower Ward

The Hermitage

By that time, though, the invention of gunpowder had made Mont Orgueil Castle vulnerable to attack and in 1550 the Privy Council ordered the States to "make a bulwark" on L'Islet. Little was done, however, until the reign of Queen Elizabeth when the military engineer Paul Ivy was put in charge and the Upper Ward or Keep of the fortress was constructed, as was the Governor's House in which Jersey's most famous Governor, Sir Walter Raleigh, took up residence in 1600. He christened the castle Fort Isabella Bellissima (Elizabeth the Most Beautiful), a name immediately shortened to Elizabeth Castle.

Sir Philippe de Carteret trebled the castle's size in Charles I's reign by enclosing the ground containing the monastery. This took ten years which Sir Philippe blamed on "the slothfulness of the workmen" but only seven years later, when Civil War broke out, the castle proved its worth and Sir Philippe was able to withstand a siege by the Parliamentarian Lieutenant-Governor Major Lydcott, and wait for his nephew, Captain George Carteret, to recover the Island for the king. The 15-year-old Prince of Wales (later Charles II) stayed at the castle in 1646, along with 300 retainers. This caused a great deal of excitement in the Island and although the influx of his followers was a great strain, all were reluctant to see him go when he left to join his mother in Paris.

A year later George Carteret built Fort Charles on a rocky out-crop at the northern end of L'Islet and in 1649 Charles returned, this time as King (in Jersey only as Parliament had abolished the monarchy) and remained for twenty weeks. During his stay he performed for the first time the form of faith-healing known as the touching for the King's Evil – apparently curing 24 people of the skin disease scrofula. This medieval ritual was revived by Charles, for obvious political reasons, and after the Restoration he is said to have cured 90,000 sufferers in London.

The King eventually left to invade England through Scotland, but his army was crushed at the Battle of Worcester by Cromwell, who then turned his attention to Jersey. In 1651 Admiral Blake and his Parliamentary forces landed in St. Ouen's Bay (see page 55) and Sir George Carteret prepared for a long siege much like his uncle's. Before long, however, a mortar bomb demolished the Abbey, ignited the supply of gunpowder and destroyed two thirds of the Castle's provisions. This disaster forced Carteret to surrender and for the next nine years the Parliamentarians held the Island. Today, all that remains of the Abbey is a modern granite cross marking the position of the high altar.

After the restoration the whole islet was enclosed with walls and twice during the 18th century unpopular leaders took refuge there. During de Rullecourt's raid of 1781 (see St. Helier, Royal Square and Grouville la Roque), the guns were again fired in anger when Captain Mulcaster used them to sound the alarm, and one cannon ball took the leg off a French officer.

In 1922 the British Government handed the Castle over to the States of Jersey as an historical monument but during the Occupation the Germans brought it up to date with guns, searchlights, bunkers and a fire control tower on the roof of the Upper Keep.

After the Liberation the Castle was again taken over by the States and it is now a most interesting place to visit, with tableaux depicting some of the historic scenes, a Militia museum and a German Military museum. The 18th century Castle bell is rung half an hour before the causeway is due to be covered by the incoming tide, but if visitors are still engrossed, there are always the "D.U.K.W.'s" to transport them safely back to St. Helier.

Entrance to Lower Ward

The Castle from West Park

FIRST TOWER

Bus routes 6, 7, 8, 9, 9a, 12, 12a, 14, 15, 17.

This western suburb of St. Helier takes its name from the round tower which stands on the seaward side of St. Aubin's Road. In 1778 General Conway, the Governor of the day, decided to build thirty defensive towers around the island. Although these towers are usually called martello towers, most of them – including First Tower – were built before the Royal Navy attacked the round tower at Mortella Point in Corsica from whence the name came. They are also of a different design. First Tower was built around 1780 and in 1797 was manned by a sergeant, a corporal and ten men from the Royal Invalid Battalion. At one time a windmill and cistern were installed on the tower to water the trees along Victoria Avenue, but these days it simply acts as a sewer vent.

Ville-es-Nouaux

St. Andrew's Church

White Lodge

Across St. Aubin's Road from the tower is First Tower Park. Here, inside some railings and surrounded by evergreen oak trees, are the prehistoric monuments known as Ville-es-Nouaux. These consist of a Neolithic gallery grave, a Bronze Age cist and an early Iron Age site.

The gallery grave is important to archaeologists because of its long period of use as a sacred burial place. For some 2,200 years it was known, used and returned to by successive peoples. What a pity, though, that so much was lost by early pillaging and exploration, before modern experts had a chance to unearth more evidence.

In this century this grave was excavated on two levels. On the lower level limpet shells and some pottery were discovered, all on a bed of flat beach pebbles, while on the upper floor, which was paved at both ends, were found about a dozen beakers, some of which were decorated, dating from the late Neolithic period. Why beakers are found in these graves is not entirely certain. Their presence must have had more significance than just containers of provisions for the next world, as they were often empty and laid on their sides. An archer's stone wrist-guard was also found here, on earth stained from what is thought to have been decomposed bone. These tombs were for communal use, unlike the later Bronze Age cists which were for single burials or cremations. The cist on this site was originally covered by a bell-shaped mound of clay. It was found to be undisturbed, but empty. Another small cist was on this site, and was recorded by the excavators as standing on a bed of ashes and burnt earth. Its date could coincide with that of the urnfield which contained ashes and a group of cremation urns, some containing burnt remains.

Also in the park is an imaginative modern play-park and St. Andrew's Church, built in 1926. If the park is left by the path above the church leading into Mont Cochon, some amusement can be found in reading the religious graffiti on the walls of White Lodge.

ST. LAWRENCE

T he valleys and their brooks are the main attraction in this central parish which has only a mile of coastline from Millbrook to Bel Royal.

Apart from its coastal strip, this is essentially a rural parish. There are four manors – Le Colombier, Hamptonne, Handois and Avranches. The first two possess colombiers (dove-cots) that can be seen from the road. The one at Le Colombier was rebuilt in 1669 and that at Hamptonne, where permission was given to build a square colombier in 1445 was rebuilt in 1674, still with the rare square design.

A nother unusual feature is the siting of the church, Parish Hall, school and arsenal. Although built at different times these are all positioned in a straight line which is unique in the Island.

Those wishing to see a farm where carnations are grown commercially can visit Retreat Farm Nursery which exports about two million carnations each year.

Mr Len Pipon breezing in his field in St. Lawrence

CORONATION PARK – MILLBROOK

The sunken garden

Bus Routes: 8, 9, 9a, 12, 12a, 14, 15, 17

Parking
Suitable for disabled
Refreshments

Below and right: St. Matthew's and one of the fine examples of Lalique glass work

Coronation Park at Millbrook was laid out by Florence, Lady Trent and given to the island in 1937 on condition that it was maintained as a resting place for the aged and a place of recreation for the young. These conditions have been carried out to the letter, although traffic noise from both Victoria Avenue and St. Aubin's Road could disturb people's rest. A large shelter has been erected offering a panoramic view of the gardens and St. Aubin's Bay, and there is a rose-garden here, as well as a rockery and wide herbaceous borders. For the children there is a safe paddling pond and an exciting play-park, and in 1979, the International Year of the Child, a venture playground for the disabled was erected. Children find this park a continuing delight, while there is plenty to interest the horticulturally-minded adult.

Above: Venture playground at Millbrook Park
Below: The Altar of St. Matthew's Church

In 1840 the area between Victoria Avenue and the inner road consisted of sand-dunes and scrub land, but there were, by that time, enough people living in the area to warrant a church, so a country chapel-of-ease was built to save people the long walk up to the parish church of St. Lawrence. In 1934 Florence, Lady Trent, who lived at Villa Millbrook on the other side of St. Aubin's Road, conceived the idea of renovating this simple church as a memorial to her husband, the first Baron Trent of Nottingham, who as Jesse Boot was the founder of Boots chemist shops. A.B. Grayson was the architect and René Lalique, the famous glass-worker from Paris was engaged, making this the only church he decorated throughout. The twelve-foot high cross, the communion rail and the screens dividing the Lady Chapel and the vestry from the Chancel are all of glass decorated with Jersey and madonna lilies are symbols of purity. The font is the only one made from glass in the British Isles, and possibly the world. There is a group of four angels behind the alter in the Lady Chapel, and these, together with the cross and the glass pillars, are illuminated when the church is in use.

Two more glass angels stand by the entrance, and the tall windows are also made of the same slightly opaque material. Interest in this church is perhaps enhanced by the fact that when Lalique died, his formula for making this glass was lost.

WATERWORKS VALLEY

This valley is more reminiscent of a Scottish glen than a Jersey valley because of the three reservoirs that have been built over the last hundred years. Before that, though, it looked very different because the stream was swift enough to power six if not seven water mills including a paper mill and the Moulin à Sucre which crushed sugar.

During the nineteenth century, when the advent of steam had made the mills obsolete and the rapid growth in the population of St. Helier had made the old system of street pumps inadequate, it was decided that all this water should be used to supply the town. The first attempt went badly wrong, but in 1882 the Jersey New Waterworks Company was formed and it was they who built the reservoirs; Millbrook in 1898, Dannemarche in 1909 and Handois (on the site of old china clay quarries) in 1932. The jersey Fresh Water Angling Association have fishing rights in both Millbrook and Dannemarche where there are good supplies of fish such as carp and tench.

Fishing at Dannemarche reservoir

Walking is pleasant in this valley – even the main road, Chemin des Moulins, is not busy and can easily be reached on foot from any of the lanes leading from La Grande Route de St. Laurent and La Route de St. Jean (Mont Cochon).

One footpath owned by the parish can be found just off Ruelle de St. Clair. After turning onto that road off Mont Cochon, take the grassy track to the right between two private drives. This followed the course of a brook and used to be wet and overgrown, but is now well maintained by the parish. At the bottom can be seen the site of the écluse or mill pond of Moulin à Sucre and on the right there are various paths eventually leading past the site of Vicart Mill. On reaching the road turn left and walk back until the left hand junction with Ruelle de St. Clair. Just opposite is an abreuvoir built by a Constable Voisin at the turn of the century for the use of horses carting the granite to build the sea-wall round St. Aubin's Bay. After a stroll alongside Millbrook Reservoir return to Mont Cochon up Ruelle de St. Clair — turning from time to time to admire the view.

In mentioning all the roads leading to Waterworks Valley, one should not omit Jersey's best ghost story, set in just one of those lanes. At midnight on a certain date, it is said that wedding bells are heard and a coach with six grey horses appears. Inside is a bride, but as she approaches it can be seen that she has no face – only a grinning skull. This is apparently the ghost of a girl who committed suicide after being jilted on her wedding day. The story goes that every year, on the anniversary of that fateful day, she can be seen searching for her missing fiancé.

Dannemarche reservoir

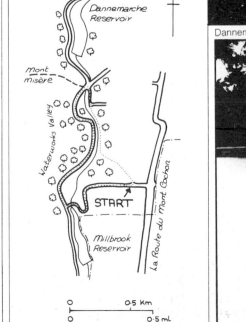

LE RÂT COTTAGE AND MOREL FARM

Bus Routes: 7, 7b

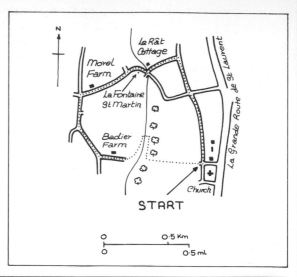

Tucked away in what must be one of the most attractive inland areas of the Island are several interesting properties belonging to the National Trust for Jersey. The easiest way of finding them is by walking from St Lawrence's Church. Take the lane to the north of the church and when you reach the T-junction turn right, and then take the second turning left. At the foot of this lane on the right hand side is Le Rât Cottage. This is a fine example of a small and fairly humble seventeenth century dwelling which, because it is owned by the National Trust, will always be preserved. The property includes the meadow to the west.

Le Rât Cottage

Turning to the right past the cottage, you will see an old cattle trough or abreuvoir originally built as a washing place, or lavoir in the 17th century. The water comes from the brook in the meadow, through a hole in the wall into the trough, and then back under the wall again and along the meadow. Almost opposite, on the other side of the road, is La Fontaine de St. Martin. This is reputed to be one of the old sacred springs and the water is said to have healing properties. Behind the spring are two small wooded côtils which also belong to the National Trust. It is possible to walk through the larger of the two, Le Côtil de la Qualité, returning along the lane below. The gurgling of the brook, the occasional duck breaking cover and the rattle of the cows' chain tethers are usually the only sounds disturbing the absolute quiet of this picturesque little valley.

A walk up the lane to the west, past the spring and the abreuvoir, eventually brings one to Morel Farm – yet another property belonging to the National Trust. The encircling wall is older than the 18th century farm house and the double roadside arch is one of the most perfectly proportioned in the Island. The main arch bears the date 1666 and the initials R. L. G. and the pedestrian arch is inscribed with a fleur de lys emblem and the initials M. L. G. These probably represent Raulin Langlois who died in 1675 and his son Matthew. On the central

La Fontaine de St. Martin

Meadows alongside Le Côtil de la Qualité

Date stone at Morel Farm

Another building of interest is the bake-house. It has been suggested that this is the original house, although there are no date stones to prove it. The bread oven and the bacon hooks are still there, as is a rough open hearth. On the south gable is a dummy chimney with pigeon holes in its southern face, and pig sties are incorporated into the building in such a way as to keep them warm but unobtrusive! This is the only known instance in Jersey of sties built in this way.

A much later building in the courtyard in front of the house has a small belfrey with a ship's bell inscribed John Morel 1837.

Although the name Morel appears in Jersey from very early times, it is believed by present members of the family that Nicolas Morel, who escaped to Jersey from France after the Massacre of St Bartholomew in 1572, was the first of their ancestors in the Island. He married Marguerite Langlois from St Lawrence. However the Langlois initials on the arches and the central chimney stack mean that the Morel family did not own the farm from the time of that original marriage.

In the 1970s a film *Neither the Sea Nor the Sand* based on a book by Gordon Honeycombe, was made in Jersey. In it this fine example of a Jersey farmhouse was placed in Scotland: a licence which caused many a smile.

An alternative route back to the church is to turn left into Les Charrières de Malorey above the farm. When the road curves to the right keep straight on into Le Chemin des Montagnes and then turn left past Badier Farm into a track which crosses the valley and eventually leads back to La Route de L'Eglise – the road behind the church.

chimney stack of the house is the date 1716 with the initials P.L.G. – perhaps Philip Langlois, son of Matthew, born in 1686.

To the right of the pedestrian arch is a mounting block, and inside is a cobbled courtyard – a rare sight in Jersey.

Although small, this is still a working farm, with a herd of cows and some rare Golden Guernsey goats, so it is not always convenient to look round. When he is available though, the tenant Mr Syd Poingdestre is happy to show people the outbuildings.

The press-house, for example, which contains a cider press and apple crusher. Each year in October or November Mr Poingdestre turns the clock back and makes his own cider. Apples are tipped into the stone crusher and a horse is led round, pulling the wheel which crushes the apples. Then the pulp is transferred to the 150-year-old press and the top screwed down until all the juice is squeezed out of the pulp. This is then transferred into a 40-gallon barrel where fermentation takes place. After a few weeks the delicious drink is ready for consumption.

Morel Farm

GERMAN MILITARY UNDERGROUND HOSPITAL

Bus Route: 8

Above: Main entrance, below: Hospital ward and operating theatre

This enormous tunnel complex should be considered in two ways – as a tremendous engineering achievement and as a memorial to all those who suffered or died during the five years of German occupation. By understanding one it is easier to comprehend the other.

The name is misleading as the complex was originally built as an artillery barracks, but in 1943 the Germans decided to convert it into a first aid field bunker as an emergency stand-by if the Island came under attack. By the Liberation the work was just about completed – the wards were ready to accommodate 500 emergency patients, the operating theatre ready for use and the kitchen gleaming with brand new equipment (which was immediately utilised by the States after the Liberation in order to feed a large number of immigrant tomato packers). The electricity was connected to the main grid, but there was also a stand-by diesel motor (that too had its uses later and was a stand-by at the General Hospital until the 80s when it was moved to Elizabeth Castle). There were air locks in case of a gas attack, an escape shaft, a ventilation plant, a telephone exchange, doctor's quarters, a fully equipped dispensary and long corridors – all of which had to be tunnelled out of solid rock. About 14,000 tons of rock were excavated giving a floor space of 27,611 square feet and 4,000 tons of concrete was used to line the galleries. Quite a feat – but at what cost?

Although the building work was first carried out by a Pioneer battalion of the German army, at the beginning of 1942 the Organisation Todt was called in to undertake the work with its force of volunteers, forced labour and slave labour.

Unemployed Moroccans and Algerians from France were the first to arrive, quickly followed by Spanish and Jewish prisoners. Then came the Russians who, as prisoners-of-war, had been marched across Europe and arrived already half-starved and ill-shod.

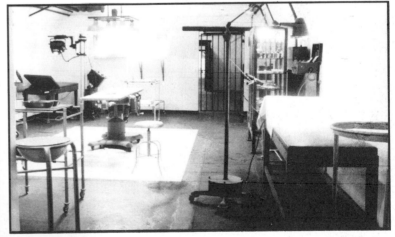

Price Code A
Open Mid-March–early
November 9.30-5.30
(last admission 5 o'clock)
Winter: Thursdays and
Sundays 2.00-5.00.
(last admission 4.15)
Closed 3 weeks in January.
Parking
Suitable for disabled
Refreshments nearby

One of the unfinished tunnels

Much has been written about the unspeakable hardships of the slaves – and it is easy to imagine the enforced misery of that arduous work on starvation rations. The forced labourers were slightly better off, but none – not even the German overseers – escaped death when tunnels collapsed.

When exploring the many rooms, exhibitions and corridors, spend time in the kitchen where a collection of letters, photographs and press-cuttings relate more vividly than any article the bravery, tragedy, sorrow and sometimes death experienced by Islanders and other nationalities alike during those years.

And on the way out, pause at the unfinished section of tunnel – and just imagine . . .

ST. BRELADE

This, the second largest parish, has the longest coastline with some of the prettiest beaches. Two not mentioned in the following pages are Belcroute Bay, which is particularly sheltered and at its best at low tide, and Beauport which is well worth the long descent. St. Brelade has the Island's second largest shopping centre at Les Quennevais and a fine 18-hole golf course at La Moye Golf Club which is situated on the sand dunes of Les Blanches Banques (described in the St. Ouen's Bay section).

Two other places of possible interest to visitors are the Belle Vue Pleasure Park with its Go-Kart track, miniature railway etc. and the Shell Garden at Seven Oaks – the creation of Mr Colin Soudain who, since 1957, has been decorating his garden in a novel way with around three million shells (entrance 20 pence).

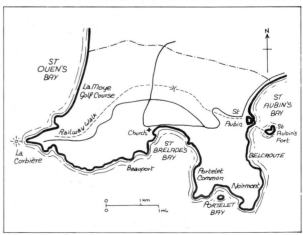

Beauport Bay

K

The ammunition store in the tunnel was protected from a possible Allied attack by a blast wall to the south, and by peering through the gates to the tunnel, one can still see the metre gauge railway line set in concrete as well as the narrow gauge track which they used internally. The Germans re-opened the railway line and as the tunnel was otherwise utilised, the original 1884 track round the hill was used again – with all its disadvantages.

Tunnel at St. Aubin

track from St. Aubin to La ... popular walk, either in its ... time, and can be started at ... the intersections along the ... opened – as far as La Moye, in 1884, but ... nected to the St. Helier – St. Aubin line until the following year. In the 1890s the line was extended to Corbière and in December 1898 a tunnel was cut into the hill at the foot of Mont Les Vaux, the reason being that the amount of coal needed for the trains to negotiate the steep bends round it had proved very costly.

This tunnel, which is at the start of the walk, is of great interest. During the 2nd World War the Germans used it to store ammunition and enlarged it by digging deep into the cliff – making a tunnel complex about the size of the German Underground Hospital. The rock from these excavations was first dumped in the harbour, but following orders from the German Navy, the Organisation Todt removed it, with the use of a narrow gauge railway, and dumped it on the beach behind the Royal Channel Island Yacht Club. There this rubble remains, spoiling what used to be a popular, sandy beach.

The walk to Corbière is varied and interesting, with the character changing constantly. The St. Aubin end is a mass of colour at all seasons with many species of flowering shrubs and plants whereas at the other end pine trees line the route, pervading the air with their bitter-sweet scent.

A play park at Les Quennevais is a welcome stop for children, and at La Moye, the view over the golf course and sand-dunes to the wide sweep of St. Ouen's Bay is magnificent.

There are plenty of seats along the way, steps up to Les Quennevais and a bus stop just by the old terminus at Corbière.

Before the return journey, by foot, car or bus, note the large slab of deep red granite set close by the terminus building. This is La Table des Marthes – a survivor from a lost megalithic structure. Its name could mean "witnesses table" as before 1850 any contracts signed on the stone were held to be particularly binding. It has also been said that the name comes from the game "le jeu des Martes" (knuckle bones) which could have been played on the flat surface.

Table des Marthes

VISIT

The Cobweb

LA VALEUSE   ST. BRELADE'S BAY   TEL: 42202

FOR:

MORNING COFFEES
LIGHT LUNCHES
AFTERNOON TEAS
RENOWNED FOR **JERSEY CREAM TEAS**
SERVED IN THE PICTURESQUE, SHELTERED OLDE-WORLDE TEA
GARDENS, OR IN THE STABLE-ROOM & CONSERVATORY.
HOME-MADE CAKES AND SCONES OUR SPECIALITY.

ALSO

THE COBWEB SHOP AT THE TOP OF THE TEA-GARDEN
WHERE YOU CAN TAKE HOME SOMETHING SPECIAL FROM OUR
MOUTH-WATERING SELECTION OF CAKES, PIES, ETC.
OUTSIDE CATERING ON REQUEST, COCKTAIL PARTIES A SPECIALITY.

YOU'LL FIND US HERE

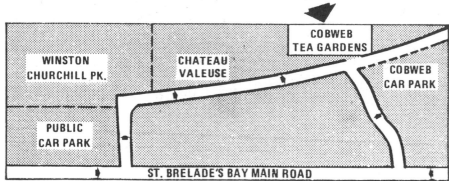

ST. AUBIN

With Noirmont Point providing the shelter from the prevalent south-westerly gales, this was, for centuries, the safest anchorage for shipping. Strangely, though, no mention was made of St. Aubin until the 16th century, and as it had no church until the 18th century how it came by its name is a mystery – although as this saint was said to give protection against pirates, the name seems to have been a happy choice for an undefended village.

Defence came in 1542 in the form of a squat one-storeyed tower built on the islet which was fortified by bastions a few years later. Over the centuries it was strengthened and remodelled and its present appearance dates from 1840 when it was reconstructed. As with most other early fortifications the Germans utilised St. Aubin's Fort, adding ferro-concrete casements and tank-turret guns. It is now used as a youth activities centre.

As to the harbour – in the 17th century when the Newfoundland cod-fishing industry was booming, it was felt that a pier should be built. In 1649 Charles II offered 500 pistoles (about £165) towards this and twenty years later he ordered that part of the import duties should be used for the purpose. The first pier, projecting from the Fort, was built in 1675 although the present south pier was not begun until 1754 and the north pier not built until 1816.

Merchants, wanting to be on the spot when their ships arrived, built spacious houses with large cellars to store the goods. In 1685 Dumaresq wrote "The conveniency of the pier has occasioned a small town to be built, consisting of about four-score houses" and by the 18th century it was a prosperous community – hence the need for a church of its own. A chapel-of-ease was eventually built, but that was condemned as unsafe in 1887 and the present church was built in 1892.

As early as 1584 there was a market in St. Aubin, and as the town grew in importance, so did the need for a bigger and better market. In 1772 a new one was erected and in 1826 a bigger one still was opened, the money for the building having been raised by four lotteries.

St. Aubin's Harbour

Bus routes 12, 12a, 15

St. Brelade's Parish Hall

As St. Helier's harbour grew, it drew the shipping away from St. Aubin, and as transport to the capital became easier, there was less need for a market, which gradually fell into disuse. A modern but faithful reconstruction on the site now houses the National Westminster Bank.

St. Aubin emerged from the 18th century as a wealthy little community, but very much cut off from the growing town of St. Helier, the only route to which was across the sand at low tide. Even when General Don's military road was built in 1810 it stopped at La Haule and the extension road to the harbour was not completed until 1844.

Although a railway for the Island was discussed as early as 1845, it was not until 1870 that amid great celebrations, the first train ran from St. Helier to St. Aubin, and it was to be another fourteen years before the line to La Moye – and subsequently to La Corbière – was opened.

The coming of rail transport proved to be a mixed blessing for St. Aubin. The Company acquired and demolished what remained of Le Moulin d'Egoutte Pluye (Raindrop Mill) which for centuries had served the area, and the western half of the market was also destroyed to allow the two railway lines to be connected.

The railway had a chequered history. In the early days it constantly ran into financial problems, and although it ran successfully during the first two decades of this century (for example carrying over a million passengers in 1925), competition from buses and coaches finally proved too much. It eventually closed in 1936 after a disastrous fire at St. Aubin, which destroyed most of the rolling stock.

All that remains of the railway buildings in the town is the Terminus Hotel which, since 1948, has been the parish hall of St. Brelade.

St. Aubin has retained a certain charm with its steep streets and its old houses. Those built on the Bulwarks – or Le Boulevard – are among the oldest and the Old Court House (recognised by many as "The Old Barge" in the BBC Television "Bergerac" series), is of particular interest. It is generally thought that this house, which for many years was the tallest in the Island, was the venue for the auctions of the prizes brought in by privateers. Who knows how many other houses in the town were built from the proceeds of that 17th century legalised piracy.

High Street, St. Aubin

ST. BRELADE'S BAY

Bus route 12

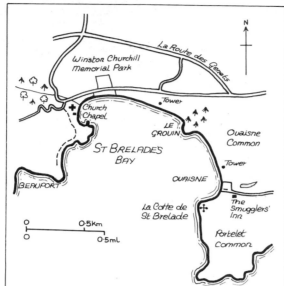

"You who love Nature in her wildest beauty . . . come to St. Brelade's and you will find the object of your search." That was how an 1844 guide-book chose to describe this bay whose remoteness made it a favourite place for smuggling.

Although that guide-book compiler would hardly recognise the bay now, with its hotels and houses, its sun-worshippers and wind-surfers, there are still places to explore "far from the madding crowd".

To the south-west of the main beach, for example, is an old stone stone jetty which can be reached at low tide, and beyond that are some steps leading to Le Coleron, a National Trust property on a small headland which is the site of one of the batteries built to defend the area when it was thought to be vulnerable to attack from the French. Another battery was placed at Le Frét point at the southern end of Portelet Common and two round towers were built in the bay. Le Coleron can also be reached by the road leading between the church and the new cemetery, and further along this road, on the hillside, there is the tomb of Jesse Boot, 1st Baron Trent of Nottingham, who founded the Boot's chain of chemist shops, and whose family gave so much to the Island.

St. Brelade's Bay

St. Brelade's Harbour

The parish church has the most picturesque setting, and to explain its presence in such a previously isolated area a legend grew up that when it was being built in a more convenient place, the devil removed the stones by night to their present position. In fact there are many examples of such chapels in the U.K. and Europe, and that legend is common to most of them.

The church is named after St. Brelade, or Bren Gwaladr who, it is said, was a companion of St. Sampson, Bishop of Dol, who landed in Jersey in the 6th century. It is a very good example of a Norman church outline, with both chancel and nave pre-dating 1066, although the aisle and windows were added much later. The Fishermen's Chapel, built alongside, was probably built by a wealthy family. It has some fine 14th and 15th century wall paintings including "Man's Redemption" and "The Last Judgement" with the Virgin Mary very much in evidence. Restoration work is being undertaken on this chapel, and details of guided tours are posted on the church notice-board.

Before the Reformation all parish churches had Perquage paths to allow criminals who had taken sanctuary within the church to escape the Island. According to the law they could stay in the church and be provided with food for nine days. After that they were forced to swear to leave the Island for ever and were led direct to the sea. St. Brelade has the shortest Perquage path.

Fishermans' Chapel

The Winston Churchill Memorial Park, opened in 1966, is beautifully laid out with spacious lawns, flower-beds, fountains, a waterfall and steep wooded paths. This park has a large granite dedication stone bearing the head of Churchill and the inscription "The Right Honourable Winston Spencer Churchill K.G., O.M., C.H. 'and our dear Channel Islands are also to be freed today".

Round Tower Ouaisné

Winston Churchill Memorial Park

healthy population has successfully bred in Jersey for many years. Ouaisné Common (La Commune de Bas) is one of the bird's strongholds and as this small and attractive insect-eating bird is non-migratory, it can be seen here throughout the year. The marshy pond on the common is also the best breeding ground for Jersey's only species of frog, the agile frog *Rana dalmatina*. Unfortunately this rare amphibian has become an endangered species, unlike the crapaud (toad) which is relatively common. It is worth remembering that the spawn of the toad is just as interesting and is plentiful enough to collect without putting the future of a species at risk.

Le Grouin Headland

Le Grouin is a headland planted with pine and cypress trees which divides the bay between St. Brelade and Ouaisné. Two 12-pounder guns once stood here to guard the bay against the French, and the Germans also utilised its cover to fortify the bay.

The beach on the Ouaisné side is less crowded and behind the sea wall (which stretches the whole length of the bay and was built as an anti-tank wall by the Germans) lies a large open area predominantly covered with gorse. This is a rich habitat for small birds such as the linnet, stonechat and the shy, elusive Dartford warbler which takes its English name from Dartford Heath in Kent where the species was first identified. Due to a continuous loss of habitat it no longer breeds in Dartford, but a small

Le Coleron

A steep wooded path leading off Ouaisné Hill above the Smugglers' Inn leads to La Commune de Haut or Portelet Common. This large area of heath is a delightfully quiet spot for picnics and walks and the views are incredibly beautiful. The National Trust for Jersey own a large part of the area including the site of the battery and a magazine.

Below the headland is La Cotte de St. Brelade where Palaeolithic remains were discovered. As mentioned in the introduction to this book there is no access to this cave and because quarrying used to take place around the headland, people are warned not to venture too near the edge.

Dartford Warbler
(Stentiford)

NOIRMONT POINT AND PORTELET BAY

Command Bunker

Bus route 12a
Bunker open Thursday
evenings 7-9 June to end
August and Sundays 2-5
commencing Easter
Sunday and then the first
Sunday of every month until
October.
Entrance free.

Command Bunker interior

The headland of Noirmont has been bought by the States as a permanent war memorial, which is perhaps fitting as here was built Batterie Lothringen, one of four naval artillery batteries installed in the Channel Islands following an order by Hitler in 1941 thereby forming the largest concentration of emplaced artillery in Western Europe.

During that time the whole headland was trenched so that men could move from the guns to the bunkers in comparative safety. There were searchlight installations on both sides and further inland machine guns and flame-throwers defended the point from a land attack. There were at least six gun emplacements, each with a concrete run leading to an ammunition bunker. The guns themselves were not the massive sixteen inch models originally ordered by Hitler, but medium German artillery of First World War origin. These were tipped over the cliffs by the British Forces following the Liberation in an understandable drive to remove all evidence of the occupation, but one has been retrieved from Les Landes and has been mounted here. The gunners had telephonic communication with the main command post housed in a large bunker which in itself is a feat of engineering. Steel-lined and made of solid concrete, it was started in March 1943 and completed in April 1944. It was built to a master design and thousands of tons of material were used. It is fortunate that in 1948 this bunker was sealed up which saved it from suffering the fate of its Guernsey and Alderney counterparts which had every bit of metal removed for scrap and were denuded of everything that could be cut away.

This was a naval establishment, so the main control centre resembles the fire control centre of a battleship. It was to this room that the gunners reported their sightings and once that information had been collated and corrected by a computer, it was from here that the fire control officer would give the necessary orders. The whole bunker was ventilated and centrally heated, and there is even a gas lock between double steel doors, the rubber seals of which are still perfect after over forty years.

In every room can be seen evidence of the self-sufficiency of this massive bunker. The general assembly room, map-lined and still with hammock hooks on the ceiling; the forty-foot escape shaft; the ventilation room which, in case of siege, would provide constant fresh air and back at the entrance, a well-protected room housing a machine gun to protect the bunker from intruders.

Portelet

At the southermost tip is La Tour de Vinde, a defensive tower built between 1810 and 1814 which is now used as a shipping marker with an unattended white light which flashes out to sea every ten seconds.

Gun emplacements

The headland offers superb views right round the south coast beyond St. Helier, and to the west can be seen the attractive beach of Portelet Bay which can be reached by a footpath and steps below the Old Portelet Inn.

To the east of Portelet is Ile Percée, a rock through which the sea has made a tunnel, and dominating the bay is Ile au Guerdain, which is often refered to as Janvrin's Tomb. In 1721 Philippe Janvrin, a St. Brelade man who was the captain of the ship *Esther* was on the homeward journey when plague broke out on board. He was forced to anchor off-shore at Belcroute, as was the custom for plague-ridden ships, and eventually he died. As his body was not allowed home for burial, his widow arranged for him to be buried on Ile au Guerdain. His body was later transferred to the cemetery at St. Brelade and ninety years after his death a Jersey round tower was erected on the island.

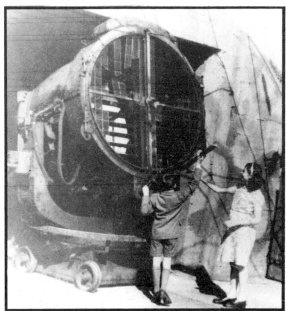

150 cm. searchlight "Max" *(R.H. Mayne)*

Also on the headland is one of three observation towers, the other two being at La Corbière and Les Landes (see page 47).

It is easy to see the strategic importance of this headland to the occupying forces, and it is due to the Channel Islands Occupation Society which has maintained the bunkers and emplacements since 1977 that this part of the Island's modern history is preserved and open to the public.

There is a network of paths on the headland and it is also possible to scramble down to the shoreline to explore the delights of the rockpools. During the last century it was suggested that a harbour be built to the east of the point towards Belcroute Bay, but the British Government chose the ill-fated St. Catherine's site instead (see page 91).

Bathing can be extremely dangerous around the natural bridge connecting Ile au Guerdain with the upper beach and in 1915 eight Jesuit students lost their lives while swimming here. However, Portelet is one of the most attractive bays in Jersey and one that is fun to explore. To the west, for example, large water-worn boulders can be seen well above the present tide-level proving that the sea level was once far higher, and in the shallow soil on the western headland, flint implements of Early Man are often found.

LA CORBIERE

Bus route 12

Observation Tower, now "Jersey Radio"

The views from this rocky promontory are legendary and are particularly spectacular at sunset or when a strong westerly gale is blowing and the sea is beating against the rocks. It is then that one realises that the place is well-named, for the word Corbière is derived from "corbeau" – a crow, which used to be considered a bird of ill-omen, and the records tell us that for hundreds of years ships have been wrecked on these rocks. In 1414 for example, a Spanish ship was lost and "the sands of St. Ouen's Bay were strewn with casks of wine". Also the great sand-storm of St. Catherine's Day 1495 (see St. Ouen's Bay Les Blanches Banques), was attributed to God's wrath at the cruelty shown to the crews of five Spanish caravels wrecked on the rocks. Over the centuries the toll continued to rise but it was not until 1873 that the States agreed to the building of a lighthouse.

A rock 500 yards from the shore was chosen as the site by the engineer Imrie Bell, and Sir John Goode designed the lighthouse, the first in the British Isles to be constructed in concrete. It is now unmanned. The electric light can be seen for eighteen miles in good visibility and, when needed, the fog-horn blasts for five seconds in every minute.

The lighthouse can be reached by foot at low tide, but visitors are warned that the incoming tide is extremely dangerous. A memorial stone at the entrance to the causeway reads "Peter Larbalestier, assistant keeper at the lighthouse who on the 28th May 1946 gave his life in attempting to rescue a visitor cut off by the incoming tide. Take heed all ye that pass by!"

M ounted in a casement nearby is a 10.5 cm French field gun captured by the Germans in 1940 and converted for fortress use. There were 84

German bunker

such guns in the Channel Islands, but now only five remain – all in Jersey.

To the east can be seen one of three observation towers built by the Germans during the occupation – the others being at Noirmont and Les Landes. 5,000 bags of cement were used to build each of these towers which had a view across the whole Gulf of St. Malo, and from where the men could communicate by telephone with the Artillery Communications bunker at St. Peter which in turn could report to the Corps Headquarters at St. Lô. This particular tower is now used by the Harbour Office as the ship-to-shore communications centre, Jersey Radio.

F urther still to the east is the little cove of La Rosière, which can be reached by a path next to the Highlands Hotel. It is generally thought that this inaccessible spot was once well used by smugglers. There are several caves nearby, and one particularly deep one, known as Smugglers' Cave, is just to the east of the beach and can be entered and explored at low tide.

Nearby is the desalination plant, commissioned in 1970, but only used when there is an acute water shortage.

ST. PETER

The most obvious landmark in this parish is the Airport, opened in 1937 at a cost of £128,000 and now greatly extended. The promenade decks are open to the public free of charge. An interesting relic from a much earlier age is the Tudor cannon at the bottom of Beaumont Hill inscribed *John Owen made this pese anno dni 1551 for the Paryshe of Saynt Peter in Jersse.*

The parish church is one of eight known to have existed before 1066 and, still on a religious note, the base of a medieval wayside cross can be seen at the top of Jubilee Hill – the cross itself having been destroyed by 16th century reformers.

The windmill in the north was originally built in 1837. It has been restored very much to its original style, complete with sails, and is now a public house.

As the parish extends down to St. Ouen's Bay, places of interest can also be found under that section.

Tudor Cannon on Beaumont Hill

VAL DE LA MARE RESERVOIR WALK

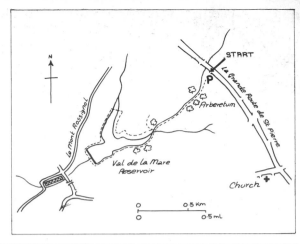

Bus routes 9, 9a

A new and beautiful country walk came into being with the creation of the New Waterworks Company's Val de la Mare reservoir. This is the largest in the Island, with a capacity of 207 million gallons of water and it is now possible to walk round its Y-shaped boundaries, which straddle the parishes of St. Peter and St. Ouen, on paths that are well-maintained, and which offer unusual views.

The start of the walk is on the route of the German built railway-line from La Pulente to Ronez Quarry. This line was apparently opened but only used for a short time. On the main road by the car park there still exists the bridge built to allow the trains to run below the road.

On the left-hand side of the path leading to the reservoir, can be seen an unusual arboretum opened in 1977 at the instigation of the organisation Trees for People. Here the Public Works Department are planting trees from different regions of the world, set out in separate sections. The Australasian area was the first to be planted followed by that of North America. There is an area of Mexican pines to the right and further areas will be developed over the coming years.

As one reaches the north-eastern tip of water there is another footpath to the right which leads up La Rue de Coin, down Les Charrières and so up to Mont Rossignol via Le Chemin du Soudard, but for the circular reservoir walk keep to the main path with the water on your right until the dam is reached. This is 535 feet along the crest and 75 feet high from the valley floor and contains 52,000 cubic yards of concrete in its 26 articulated blocks. When, in 1962, the Home Secretary of the day, R.A. Butler, officially closed the scour valve, the raw water storage capacity of the Island was effectively doubled. However the dam has not been without its problems. In 1971 it became the first structure in the British Isles in which a concrete deterioration known as Alkali Aggregate Reactivity was identified and there has also been a suggestion of some local seismic activity in the valley bottom, so work is continually going on to monitor the performance of the structure and seismometers have been added to the impressive array of instruments used by the Jersey New Waterworks Company.

None of this need concern the pedestrian. The walk leads down to the valley below the dam, the site of the old water mill Le Moulin de la Mare, and up the other side. It then keeps to the Y-shape of the reservoir, up the north-west arm, keeping to the water's edge, across a small dam and, on the raised ground between the two arms of water, down the other side and so up to the northern side of the eastern arm until the original path is met at the north-eastern tip.

This is a pleasant and varied walk that will be enjoyed by adults and children alike.

ST. PETER'S VALLEY

St. Peter's Valley from Mont des Louannes

Bus route 8.

Perquage at Goose Green

Tesson Chapel

In 1859, when Queen Victoria visited Jersey for the second time, her A.D.C., Sir John Le Couteur decided that a drive through this valley would offer the prettiest views for Her Majesty. The valley is still beautiful, especially in spring when thousands of wild daffodils carpet the hillsides and later, when yellow iris flower in abundance along the course of the stream.

The German occupation left scars: they built a power station at Tesson Mill, along with a reservoir used for cooling purposes. Three enormous ammunition tunnels as well as many other cross tunnels were driven deep into the hillside, disgorging thousands of tons of stone and rubble – some of which was used in the construction of the airport runway in 1952.

Command Bunker

St. Peter' Valley stream served eight mills at one time or another. There is a walk through National Trust property from Tesson Mill which winds its way along wooded côtils until it turns to the right, and after crossing the stream by way of a wooden bridge, leads back to the main road.

The Perquage paths from the churches of St. Mary, St. John and St. Lawrence meet at Tesson Chapel, and then this joint pre-Reformation sanctuary path wends its way through Goose Green Marsh to reach the sea at Beaumont.

The Fantastic Tropical Gardens which closed in 1981, and which had become seriously neglected, is once again open to the public. The five Oriental themes in the gardens, laid out by the original proprietor in the 1950s, are being retained, along with the many rare and exotic plants, and there are plans to add something new to the gardens each year so that they become more Fantastic as the years go by.

Another place much frequented by visitors is the Strawberry Farm, which is in the area used by the Germans during the occupation as their Battle Headquarters. Regarding this as the centre of the Island, the occupying force built three command bunkers, one of which is now open to the public at the Strawberry Farm, two communication bunkers and a water storage and pumping station, all originally painted with windows and supplied with roofs to look like conventional houses. The Farm also boasts Jersey's only "model village" with miniature reproductions of such places as Grosnez Castle, St. Mary's Forge and the Smugglers' Inn at Ouaisné. There is also a craft centre on the premises, where leather carvers, glass-blowers, jewellery workers, spinners and weavers can be seen at their work.

LE MOULIN DE QUETIVEL

Crushing grain to make meal was one of man's earliest skills. Neolithic man used stone querns for the purpose but in early medieval times water power was discovered and mills were built which operated in very much the same way as this one does today.

Le Moulin de Quétivel had already been in existence for some time before it appeared in the records of 1309 as a Crown mill. In feudal times tenants had to grind their corn at a particular mill or be subjected to a fine. They had to give every 16th sheaf to the owner and were also forced to provide labour and materials. In 1562 the Royal Commission sold the mill into private ownership and since that time it has had several owners.

By the 18th century many mill families had become as powerful as the feudal lords had once been. They controlled the price of flour, and therefore bread – a monopoly which eventually led to the "bread riots" of 1847. During the first six decades of the nineteenth century the mill owners prospered: wheat was imported from the Baltic and the flour exported across the Atlantic, but with the advent of steam power many mills were closed.

Le Moulin de Quétivel was still being worked at the end of the last century, but then fell into disrepair. During the German Occupation, along with several other mills, it was repaired and utilised. but after the war, when milling ceased, it became an agricultural store. In 1969 the National Trust for Jersey decided to preserve it, not only to grind local corn, but as a site of historical and educational importance. Unfortunately a disastrous fire delayed their plans and it was not until 1979 that the mill became fully operational once more.

The car park is situated by the mill pond (l'écluse), which with the aid of a series of sluice gates provides the water needed to work the twelve foot diameter water wheel. From there, there is a short walk above the leat, affording excellent views of the valley below.

Bus route 8
Price Code D
Open March to October,
Tuesdays and Wednesdays
10-4.
Leaflets, Guidebook
National Trust Shop

Top floor of Mill

The mill itself has been beautifully restored in a way which allows the visitor to see and understand the process of making stone-ground flour. One starts on the top floor where there is an exhibition explaining the method of milling and the history of Jersey mills, and then, armed with the explanatory leaflet, one proceeds down to the first floor and finally to ground level.

It is quite a thought that for at least 600 years a mill on this site has been providing flour for the people of Jersey, and in a small way is still doing so.

JERSEY MOTOR MUSEUM

Bus routes 9, 9a
Price Code D
Open March-October
10-5
Suitable for disabled
Guide Book

2-wheel collection

The birthday gift of a petrol-driven child's car just before the war started a love of the combustion engine that has led Michael Wilcock to be a racing driver, a Curator of Lord Montagu's Brighton Motor Museum and, since 1973, Director of this museum. The other half of the partnership is Richard Mayne, a local historian and author whose ambition had always been to start such a museum.

Of course it is the cars that take pride of place, but there are other gems to be discovered such as the 1870 railway carriage used by the Jersey Railways and subsequently used as a home by a retired stationmaster. Now, beautifully restored, it serves as a reminder of the days when even in Jersey to travel first class was to travel in great luxury.

A ride on one of the earliest bicycles – like the one made in 1886, would have been far less comfortable. This is just one of a collection which includes a penny-farthing, a Victorian tricycle and German war-time bikes.

There are motor-bikes too, including a Sunbeam S7 which was presented to Field-Marshal Montgomery in 1948, a 1939 D. K. W. used by despatch riders during the German Occupation and a 1933 Sunbeam which was successfully concealed from the Germans during that time.

The smallest cars on display are of course the children's cars including Michael Wilcock's early birthday present – a 1¼ H. P. Bentley and a 1963 Cheetah Cub Child's car based on the design of the Jaguar "D" Type sports-racing car. At the other end of the size-range is the 1942 Mack Prime Mover – a heavy Artillery Tractor which took part in the Liberation of Jersey in 1945. Although later used for heavy emergency work it was retired in 1971. Apart from being too big for Jersey roads its petrol consumption of two miles to the gallon left a lot to be desired. Still with the war, there are armoured vehicles from both sides including a V. W. Kubelwagen and a Ford Jeep – both built in 1942. The latter took part in the 1974 D-Day Memorial Tour of Normandy.

1912 Talbot 2-seater sports

Below: 1936 Rolls-Royce used in 1944 by Field-Marshal Montgomery

Early car accessories, historic photographs and Dinky toys are also displayed, as is a St. Helier fire engine, but of course the cars are the central attraction.

Enthusiasts will delight in the Racing Bentleys, the 1911 Darracq, the 1912 Talbot and the 1936 Rolls-Royce Phantom III as well as the less grand but beautifully restored 1926 Austin Seven Chummy and the Model T Ford "Tin Lizzie". The collection is large and includes many famous names. Each and every one of these beautiful machines is in full working order and it is good to know that many are used in vintage rallies.

ST. PETER'S BUNKER

German telephone and original grave cross from St. Brelade's cemetery

Enigma Machine

Bus routes 9, 9a

Price Code D
Open March-October
10-5
Guide Book

Built in 1942 by the Organization Todt, using Russian and other slave labour, this underground bunker now houses the largest collection of Nazi German equipment and Occupation relics in the Channel Islands. Its original purpose was to guard the western approach to the airport and it was the Headquarters of Machine Gun Battalion 16. The 33 men of the Battalion slept here but ate at the adjacent hotel where the officers were billeted. On the roof of the hotel was an anti-aircraft gun, and one German visitor, returning to his old bunker, reminisced that he spent many hours manning the gun on D-Day (June 6th 1944) against an invasion which, of course, never took place.

Each of the six rooms in the bunker is packed with objects of historical interest and except for a few medals that would be too valuable to display, everything is original – even the uniforms on the models and Hitler's signature.

One of the few remaining Enigma decoding machines is displayed in Room 1. These were invented to enable top secret information to be passed between strategic German positions and were thought to be invulnerable. History has shown us that this was just not so once the Allies had deciphered the codes. This particular machine was used in the film "A Man Called Intrepid" starring David Niven.

In the adjacent room among many items made from necessity by Islanders during the Occupation and near a blanket beater used as often on Russian slave-workers as on blankets, can be seen a 1940 brochure recommending Jersey as an ideal place for a war-time holiday!

Twin barrelled anti-aircraft gun

Room 3 is an actual reconstruction, using the original bunk-beds, furniture, stove and rifle rack and in Room 4 are displayed various German uniforms, caps, helmets, badges and medals.

The machine-gun room is next and in Room 6, which is the largest, can be seen the original air conditioning unit as well as German motor-cycles, figures of a Luftwaffe pilot and a Paratrooper together with a vast collection of guns, fire fighters' equipment etc.

For those who want to listen as well as look there is a twenty-minute recording giving a brief outline of the Occupation and a description of what life was like in Jersey during those difficult years. As the souvenir guide explains – this exhibition is not presented as a glorification of the paraphernalia of the Third Reich, but as a small reminder of man's inhumanity to man.

IM NAMEN DES
DEUTSCHEN
VOLKES

VERLEIHE ICH

DAS VERDIENSTKREUZ
DES ORDENS VOM DEUTSCHEN
ADLER
ERSTER STUFE

BERLIN·DEN

DER FÜHRER

DER CHEF DER ORDENSKANZLEI

STAATSMINISTER

"Order of the German Eagle" with authentic signature of Adolf Hitler

SUNSET NURSERIES

Until 1975 the two acres of greenhouses here were used for growing tomatoes, but now it has become a show-place where visitors can wander at will and learn something of the horticulture industry.

In one glass-house for example, there is a demonstration of hydroponics were one can see melons, cucumbers, tomatoes, peppers and aubergines being raised.

Further down are six glass-houses each containing 12,500 carnations grown for export and the postal-packing service run by the nurseries. Many shades of carnation are grown and the blooms at the end of each row are left on the plants for the enjoyment of the visitors.

Gerberas have to be fully open before they are picked, so the glass-house containing these exotic flowers is particularly coulouful. When packed, each of these long-lasting flowers has to be individually protected by a plastic cup.

Between February and June it is possible to see freesias being grown under glass, and as a complete contrast other areas have been put aside for raising trout and as an aviary.

The scent from jasmine in April, broom genista in May and June and stephanotis in summer hangs on the air in the Tropical Garden – a relatively new venture where many species thrive under ideal conditions.

For no extra charge one can explore the mysteries of the Passion Flower Maze. This unusual idea is based on the design of the famous Hampton Court Maze, but here the divisions are made with trellises of passion flowers — named apparently by 16th century Spanish missionaries to South Africa who felt that the flowers resembled the instruments of the Passion.

On the road outside the nurseries can be seen a bridge – this dates back to the occupation when the Germans built a railway from the granite quarries at St. John to La Pulente.

ST. OUEN'S BAY

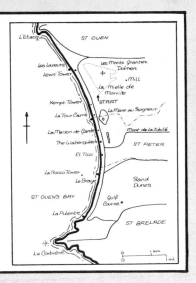

This great bay straddles three parishes, St. Brelade, St. Peter and St. Ouen.

The entire bay is so rich in places of interest that readers are advised to visit the Information Centre at Kempt Tower where guides to the coastal footpaths, birdlife, flora, archaeology and the German fortifications can be obtained, as well as advice and information regarding this very special recreation and conservation area. It is open between 2 and 4.30 during the summer and, during the winter, certain weekends.

Bus route 12a.

ST. OUEN'S BAY Beach

This five-mile stretch of sandy beach offers ample space for those who want to swim, sunbathe and "get away from it all". There are plenty of car parks and cafes along the length of the bay, and people soon find their own favourite spot. For those with young children the southern end, near Le Braye slip, is ideal whereas those who want to surf or enjoy more rigorous swimming will prefer to go further north.

In summer, surfing is confined to three separate areas, each marked with red and white signs visible from the beach. They are, roughly, the stretches near the El Tico restaurant, either side of the Watersplash and just past Kempt Tower as far as the aptly named "Barge Aground". In the winter, when the swell is suitable, the area midway between La Pulente and La Corbière is also popular.

Surfing

Sand racing

Looking towards L'Etacq

The surf can be as good as the best in the world, and attracts up to 500 surfers, a quarter of whom pursue the sport the whole year round. Local, national and international surfing championships organised by the Jersey Surf Board Club are regularly held and attract large crowds.

Another crowd puller is the sand racing organised by the Jersey Motor Cycle and Light Car Club. Part of the beach is closed for these events which are held once a fortnight during the summer months. There are classes for saloon, racing and sports cars as well as motorbikes and karts and the last event of the year incorporates a forty-lap event for cars and a triella for motor cycles. Price Code E.

Back in the realms of pre-history, Neolithic man used to farm in this bay, but the fertile land was lost when the sea level rose in the post-glacial period between 4,000 and 1,000 B.C. At certain times, usually after a violent storm remnants of a vast oak forest are exposed near L'Ouzière slipway. In 1902, during a particularly spectacular exposure, some 500 tree stumps, including oak, alder and hazel were counted.

There is also a legend of a medieval manor under the sea in the L'Etacq area, but this has never been traced. It is known, however, that from the late thirteenth century there were many decades of violent storms throughout northern Europe, and it is quite possible that the sea did reclaim land that extended out and over the present tidal areas.

During the late nineteenth and early twentieth century there was again a lengthy period of high spring tides and south-westerly gales. There was great concern over possible coastal erosion and granite sea-walls were built. These, together with the concrete anti-tank walls of the 2nd World War, protect the low-lying inland area from encroachment by the sea.

The Western Golf Range with a nine-hole course, putting and crazy golf is situated in the middle of the bay.

LES BLANCHES BANQUES

Recently described as "this last remaining wilderness in Jersey", the large area of dunes to the south of St Ouen's Bay is one of the foremost systems in Europe and among the ten largest in the British Isles. They stretch from the coast through the plain and up on to the eastern plateau, and although a large area of the plateau dunes has been developed for housing and the La Moye golf course there is still ample scope for exploration on foot.

The dune system has existed some 3,000 to 4,000 years (the oldest part being the plateau dunes since they lie inland) and Neolithic tombs and flint chipping sites believed to be about 4,000 years old have been found on Les Quennevais. There are also several menhirs (standing stones) situated on the dunes and one find from them of particular interest was a Bronze Age upright cooking pot containing limpets. This is estimated to be about 3,500 years old and its position and undamaged state suggests that a sudden sand storm must have caused its owners to flee, leaving their meal untouched. Sand storms were once a recurring problem: it is recorded that on St. Catherine's Day 1495 one destroyed the fertility of Les Quennevais (a name derived from the Jersey-French word for hemp – chènevière which used to be cultivated there) and in 1668 there is a record of land in the area being "swallowed up by the sand and abandoned by its owners".

Looking west over the bay

Menhir (standing stone)

Nowadays the risks of such sand storms are slight as during the past 300 years the dune plain has become largely stabilised by vegetation. In fact the dunes are the fourth richest in higher plant life in the British Isles. There are at least 446 species of plants growing here including some at the end of their continental range, such as Jersey thrift (*Armeria arenaria*) which grows no-where else in the British Isles. This is bigger and flowers two to three months later than the common thrift. The dunes are rich in interesting grasses. The beautiful grey hair-grass is plentiful on Les Quennevais. Marram grass, which is particularly good at binding the loose sand, flourishes on the dune plain and hare's-tail grass, only introduced from Guernsey in the 1870s, covers the bay area. Flowers such as dwarf pansy, burnet rose, Lady's bedstraw and several rare species of orchids, to name but a very few, are found here, but people are requested not to pick them, for if they do not set their seeds they will soon cease to exist.

A few years ago there was grave concern that the numbers of people using the dunes for recreational activities could destroy the vegetation and cause serious erosion. Cars were banned in 1974 and now it is felt that with careful management man's incursion, on a moderate scale, may do no great harm. On the other side on the coin "this last remaining wilderness" has a great deal to offer man.

LA MARE AU SEIGNEUR (St. Ouen's Pond)

This is the largest stretch of natural fresh water in the Island and is now owned by the National Trust for Jersey and maintained by the Société Jersiaise as a nature reserve and bird-ringing station. To the north of the pond are two fields, Le Noir Pré and Le Clos du Seigneur, which have been acquired by the National Trust for Jersey in order to preserve the natural habitat of the Jersey Orchid, *Orchis laxiflora*.

Until recently, as its name suggests, the pond was the property of the Seigneur of St. Ouen. The Seigneur at the time of the seven-year French occupation in the 15th century was Philippe de Carteret who was known to be a resistance leader. His arrest was ordered and he was almost captured while fishing in his pond. Seeing the soldiers creeping up on him, he leapt on to his horse and galloped towards his manor, but before he reached the crest of the hill another troop appeared in front of him, so he swerved towards Le Val de la Charrière, thereby forcing his mount to jump a gorge 18 feet deep and 22 feet wide. This the horse did, but when the Seigneur reached the safety of his manor the noble animal dropped dead with exhaustion. De Carteret "grieved greatly and caused it to be buried in his garden for the good service it had done" – and indeed in 1908 bones identified as being those of a late 15th century horse were found near the manor entrance.

In 1651, when Cromwell decided to mop up the resistance in Jersey, it was just to the south of the pond that Colonel James Heane's forces eventually landed. Imagine the fleet of 80 ships under Admiral Blake, feinting to land at St. Brelade, then sailing round to L'Etacq and so on for two days, while the Militia under Sir George Carteret marched to and fro in the pouring rain, trying to keep up with them. Many gave up and went home and it was no wonder that the hungry, tired and wet remainder of the demoralised troops were no match for the veterans of the New Model Army when they eventually landed at eleven o'clock at night. By morning the defending forces had fled and Carteret had withdrawn to Elizabeth Castle.

Looking west over the pond

Looking east

DEFENCES AND FORTIFICATIONS

At one time the defences of the bay were the responsibility of the parishes of St. Ouen and St. Peter, and the oldest surviving building is La Maison de Garde de St. Pierre, situated to the south of St. Ouen's Pond, the reversion of which is owned by the National Trust for Jersey. Built in 1765 to replace a guard house and magazine which had been blown up, it has a high pitched roof and is now painted white as a navigation marker.

La Maison de Garde de St. Pierre

La Tour Carrée

La Tour Carrée, or Square Fort, to the north of L'Ouzière Slip was built in 1778, just in time to help defend the Island from the Prince of Nassau's abortive attempt to land an invasion force in the bay in 1779 – just two years before the Battle of Jersey.

During the Napoleonic Wars the Bay became well defended. Nine towers, of which three remain, were built during this period, as well as batteries and boulevards. La Rocco Tower is the oldest survivor, having been built between 1795 and 1801. Situated on rocks at the southern end, this tower (which takes its name from Rocque-hou – rocky island) was damaged by German gunners who used the surrounding rocks for target practice. It would eventually have been destroyed by the sea had it not been for a successful appeal for its renovation launched in 1969.

The two other surviving towers can correctly be called Martellos as they were both built in 1832 to the English design and after the round tower at Mortella Point in Corsica had beaten off an attacking British warship. Kempt Tower, to the north of L'Ouzière Slip was named after Sir James Kempt, Master-General of the Ordnance and one of Wellington's Generals at Waterloo, and Lewis's Tower near Les Laveurs Slip was named after Colonel G.G. Lewis, who commanded the Royal Engineers in Jersey at that time. Recently rediscovered to the seaward side of Kempt Tower, and probably built at the same time, is a Battery where three 24-pounder guns were positioned.

During the 1st World War the Militia patrolled the area, but it was not until the German occupation that more defences were built. Realising that the early fortifications were in the best possible positions, they reinforced both Kempt and Lewis's Towers and it was not until 1943 that the fortress bunkers were built.

It should be remembered that not all concrete remains are of German origin. Still visible are the foundations of many summer bungalows and beach huts erected between the wars and removed by the occupying force.

The German fortifications are well documented in the Les Mielles guide, but to summarise: it is easy to see that the anti-tank walls, the strategically placed towers and bunkers, the minefields further inland and the artillery emplacements on the surrounding hills were excellent protection against the invasion . . . which of course never took place. The Les Mielles Guide to German Fortifications is available at the Interpretation Centre — 10p.

Kempt Tower – now the Information Centre

LA MIELLE DE MORVILLE

Since the war and up until a few years ago this area was an eyesore. Great quantities of sand had been removed to provide for the building industry and the pits filled with refuse, but in 1979 a programme of landscape restoration was started which transformed it into a haven for informal recreation.

La Mielle de Morville has areas for picnic parking and barbecues and a centrally placed large barbecue area is suitable for parties, free and can be booked in advance. To the east of the picnic area is a large flat field which is ideal for kite-flying, kicking a ball about or events such as tug-of-war competitions. The whole area has been designed in such a way as to allow easy walking among an abundance of wild flowers, which include tree lupins and evening primroses. Les Mielles is the habitat of a number of wild birds – some permanent residents and others wintering flocks of water birds. Clumps of grass are left uncut to allow them to hide and nest and two small reed-enclosed ponds have also been kept for such species as moorhen, coot and duck. Near one of these ponds is a ten-person hide belonging to the Royal Society for the Protection of Birds and the Young Ornithologists' Club.

For those with suitable footwear and two to three hours to spare, there is a circular walk, with way-mark signs, which encompasses the whole of this area and offers breath-taking views of the bay.

Conducted walks with an ornithological expert take place regularly — details from the Kempt Tower Interpretation Centre.

From the large barbecue area begin walking to the south. Straight ahead is a National Trust property known as Une Mielle vis-à-vis Kempt Tower (Kempt Tower is directly opposite on the other side of La Grande Route des Mielles) but our path goes east, away from the sea, across Le Chemin du Moulin and up a track marked as a foot-path. On the right can be seen an area where sand removal is still taking place, and straight ahead, on the sky-line can be seen St. Ouen's Mill (Le Moulin de la Campagne). There is a path leading to the mill, access depending on the season and weather conditions, but turn to the left. This area, which soon becomes wooded and crosses a brook, is known as Les Hanières after the galingale (in Jersey-French 'Han') which grows here. This plant, which flowers in late summer, is so strong when dried that it was used in place of hemp, for making rope, tethers and halters. Once the brook has been crossed by stepping stones there is a short climb to reach La Ville au Bas, with the farm of the same name on your left. Turn left just past the farm and the path then continues in a north-westerly direction along the ridge, giving a panoramic view across the bay. The land-marks can be identified easily from this vantage point, and from here one can imagine how the scene below may have looked in Neolithic times when a great forest stretched out into the bay.

The path now leads to another valley, Les Vaux Cuissin, where there is a sturdy bridge over yet another stream. The area round the stream has been planted with hazel, white poplar, oak and elm trees, the last having been injected against Dutch elm disease which, it is hoped, in this isolated valley will ensure their survival. The path beyond the bridge is a good place to stop and examine how well the man-managed La Mielle de Morville, so recently a scar on the landscape, blends with its backdrop of duneland.

That pause for reflection will hopefully provide the energy for the steep climb ahead which allows another fantastic view of the bay. Turning away from the sea, you will eventually reach a road, Les Chemins des Monts. Turn left into the road and about 400 metres along on the left is the National Trust property in which can be found the dolmen Des Monts, Grantez. Returning to the road a path to the left, through a valley known as Le Val és Reux, will take you back to the bay.

Alternatively continue round the valley to the north and eventually you will arrive at a cliff overlooking l'Étacq. Looking down at this little village one can see, next to the car and coach park, a triangle of land with a pond, Le Pré d'Auvergne, where the Les Mielles Committee have created a water-meadow with all the attendant flora and fauna. Again there is an alternative path down past a quarry to l'Étacq, but we take the left-hand path past granite out-crops where stonecrops, spleenwort and campions flower, and the creamy-white burnet rose scents the air with its fragrance in June and later adds deep colour with its blue-black fruits.

The path eventually leads between houses back to Le Chemin du Moulin, so named because the residents of l'Étacq used the road to take their corn to either Le Moulin de la Mare, the water-mill which used to stand at the foot of Mont Rossignol or Le Moulin de la Campagne, the windmill at the top of the hill.

A quarter of a mile walk, made interesting by the diversity of hedging, brings you to a grass track to your right. And there you are, back on the flat field. It has been a long walk, but there are always the barbecue areas – if you have come prepared.

Le Moulin de la Campagne

Common Snipe (Stentiford)

ST. OUEN

C overing the whole of the north-west corner of the Island, this is the largest parish with an area of 3,707 acres. Unlike the other parishes, it is divided not into vingtaines but cueillettes – a word derived from cueillir (to gather) and referring to the dues gathered from each district.

There are three Manors in the Parish, that of St. Ouen's and the two Manors of Vinchelez de Haut and Vinchelez de Bas situated in the beautiful and much photographed Vinchelez Lane.

S t. Ouen was a 7th century archbishop of Rouen, and the church dedicated to him was probably founded by some early Seigneur of St. Ouen, and definitely dates back to before the Norman conquest.

Note St. Ouen's Mill, now a shipping marker and the headquarters of the 18th (St. Ouen's) Scout Group, which occupies a mill site dating back to the 14th century and the surrounding fields which are still farmed in the medieval manner with strips of land separated by grass banks.

A certain independence of spirit is retained in St. Ouen's, making it a parish well worth exploring.

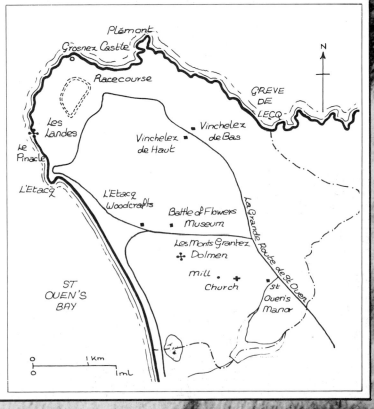

St. Ouen's Parish Church with medieval farming strips in foreground

DOLMEN DES MONTS, GRANTEZ

Bus route 9 to
St. Ouen's Church
Walking west past church,
take first turning right past
mill.
Bear left into La Rue de
Grantez and left again into Le
Chemin des Monts. ¼ mile
down this road there is a track
on the left leading up to the
dolmen.

Set in some sixty vergees, or twenty-seven acres, of land belonging to the National Trust for Jersey, this fine Neolithic passage grave was virtually undisturbed when it was investigated by the Sociéte Jersiaise in 1912, and it is easy to imagine the excitement when no less than eight skeletons were found inside, dating back some 5,000 years.

The bottle-shaped, or undifferentiated grave is about five feet below the present ground surface and was originally covered by a circular mound. It consists of a parallel-sided passage which opens out into a main chamber with a smaller side-chamber to the north. The walls are constructed of straight rectangular stones infilled with dry-stone packing. The whole tomb was originally lintelled throughout, but the main chamber is now unroofed though most of the other capstones are in place.

During the 1912 excavation seven burials were found in the main chamber, including one of a child. They were all lying in a crouched position on their sides and each interment was accompanied by quantities of limpets and the bones and teeth of ox, deer, horse, pig and goat. In addition each had received a handful of pretty sea pebbles. Another burial was found in the passage near the entrance and surrounded by a pile of stones. This skeleton was seated, with its back against the north wall, like a sentry asleep at his post.

The side-chamber, which was probably a regional variation of the more usual architecture of the time, was the only part of the tomb to have been ransacked. The capstone was found to have been cracked and there was a gap in the south wall of the tomb opposite the chamber, so it was probably entered by tunnelling or trenching from the south. Consequently no intact burials are recorded in this chamber – simply some bones and a shallow round-bottomed pottery saucer with a pair of perforations close to the rim. How lucky for posterity that these early raiders did not find the entire grave, hidden as it was under the mound.

The dolmen possibly takes its name from the Granteys family who owned land here in the 14th century. It is also sometimes known as La Pouquelaye des Monts and is the property of the Société Jersiaise who have built a protecting wall around the site.

LES LANDES

This large area of heath was once the Common of the Fief Haubert and Seigneurie of St. Ouen and is at its best in spring when the gorse is in flower and in late July when the low-growing western gorse mixes with heather to give a purple and orange carpet.

Grosnez Castle remains a mystery as no-one knows when it was built or why it was destroyed, but by 1540 it was marked in Leland's map as "Grosnes Castrum dirutum" (Grosnez Castle, destroyed). It cannot have been built much earlier than the 14th century as its corbels suggest it had a machicoulis gallery with holes in the floor for dropping stones on the enemy below – a form of defence not used before that time. It would have been useless for long sieges as it has no well, so was probably a refuge during the 14th century when the French were constantly raiding the Island. As to when it was destroyed – it could have been when du Guesclin raided the Island in 1373. A contemporary account mentions two castles (the other being Mont Orgueil) and both were eventually captured. During the French Occupation of 1461-68 the Seigneur of St. Ouen was a great resistance leader. If the castle had survived that long it could well have been then that it was dismantled by the occupying force.

During the German occupation Les Landes was an ideal location for an artillery battery. Gun emplacements, bunkers, anti-aircraft mountings and an observation tower, similar to those at La Corbière and Noirmont, still survive.

The open space of Les Landes is much in demand. There is talk of a golf course and already there is a model aircraft field and a rifle range. The race course is situated here. This replaced the Don Bridge course at Les Quennevais and is about a mile round.

Grosnez Castle from the north

German fortifications

Bus route 9a to Grosnez

Horse racing

Racing takes place eight or nine days a year and the Jersey Race Club, formed in 1981, is keen to promote the course by attracting big names such as Lester Piggott and top National Hunt jockeys.

The Meeting in May sees Europe's top lady jockeys competing, and the biggest fixture of the year is the two-day event over the August bank holiday, which attracts owners and trainers from Europe and the U.K.

Essentially, though, Les Landes is a peaceful place. Those interested in archaeology may wish to see La Hougue de Grosnez, situated to the east of the castle, although little remains of this megalithic structure. Ornithologists will be interested that short-eared owls can be seen here – but for most it will be the colour, the buttery-coconut scent of the gorse in spring, and the magnificent views of all the other Channel Islands that will be the chief attractions.

ST. OUEN'S MANOR

Bus routes 9, 9a
Price Code D
Grounds open
Tuesdays 2-6pm

There are no title deeds to this beautiful old Manor which is built in varying shades of granite including the dusky pink stone quarried from Mont Mado, for it has never been bought or sold. For nearly 850 years it has been the seat of the same family – the de Carterets, Seigneurs of St. Ouen, and we are fortunate that the present Seigneur, Philip Malet de Carteret now opens his grounds to the public once a week.

The land itself has probably been owned by the family since Viking times. The de Carterets, who had extensive properties in Normandy, may well have had a summer house here long before the Norman Conquest, although the first mention of a Manor was in 1135. The oldest surviving part is the south tower, built in 1380 when the house would have consisted of two towers and a great hall. In 1496 the Philippe of the day was given permission to fortify the Manor and in the middle to late 1500s the west and north wings were built. During the 17th century when the de Carterets were a powerful force in the Island, the Manor was again enlarged and the south and east wings added, but in the 18th century the family had grown so rich and famous that they spent most of their time at Westminster and the Manor became neglected. So it was that in 1859, when the present Seigneur's great-grandfather Colonel Malet de Carteret, inherited the property through the female line, the Manor was very dilapidated. He completely restored the interior and added the turrets on the north and west wings, the top of the central tower and the crenellations on the south tower.

Colombier (Dove-cot)

Built over so long a period and with such a wealth of history within its walls, it is not surprising that this lovely old home is known affectionately by the present Seigneur as "mystery towers" – and seeing it from the outside one can only marvel at how well all the additions blend so perfectly together.

The manorial chapel, built around the same time or earlier than the oldest part of the Manor, is dedicated to St. Anne. Desecrated by Colonel Heane's troops when the Parliamentarians successfully invaded the Island in 1651, it was used as a barn for many years but was re-dedicated in 1914.

The Manor from the north-west

The Chapel

The Altar

In March 1941 the Germans took over the Manor as a barracks and the chapel became a store-house and butcher's shop, but after the Liberation it was again re-dedicated. The altar-stone with its five crosses depicting the five wounds of Christ, is the finest in the Island. It originated from the Chapel of St. George, the Seigneurial chapel of the two Vinchelez Manors, which was destroyed during the Reformation.

The stained-glass windows are by H. T. Bosdet (1912) and depict the story of St. Anne.

Two of the sons of the Philippe who was given permission to fortify the Manor in 1496 later gained positions at the court of Henry VIII. They were apparently renowned for their prowess as athletes and the far east field became a tilting, or jousting, ground. Old documents also refer to that area as Le Jardin de la Ville de Troye, which could suggest that there was once a maze there also. The earth removed to create this area could well have been dumped into the valley below, effectively sealing off that weakness in the Manor's fortifications.

The South-east Gate-house

Amidst all the ancient history that this Manor has undoubtedly seen, one tragic episode of the Second World War is commemorated by a simple granite slab near the upper pond. It was here that 20-year-old François Scornet was executed by a firing squad after he had taken responsibility for an expedition of sixteen young Bretons who had escaped from France in a small fishing boat, SM401 Bukara, to join the Free French forces in England. Unfortunately bad weather forced them to land in Guernsey where they were promptly arrested and sent to Jersey for trial. Although three were condemned to death only young Scornet was shot. He died bravely shouting "Vive Dieu! Vive la France!" and every year, on June 18th – the anniversary of General de Gaulle's appeal to the French to join him in England – his courage is remembered by Frenchmen who make a special pilgrimage to the Manor to lay wreaths at the spot.

Placque commemorating the death of François Scornet

South side of Manor

SALLY LE GALLAIS
— Fine Arts —

SPRING — "ANTIQUES"
INCLUDING 18th CENTURY FURNITURE.

SUMMER — "PAINTINGS '83, JOHN BRATBY"
Previous Artists include: DAVID HOCKNEY, FELIKS TOPOLSKI,
PATRICK PROCKTOR, MARTIN HANDFORD, LADY MIDLETON.

AUTUMN — "SCULPTURE & GLASS"
ENZO PLAZZOTTA, CHARLIE MEAKER.

WINTER — "JEWELLERY"
GEOFFREY TURK, PETER PAGE.

OPEN DURING EXHIBITIONS 2-6 pm OR BY APPOINTMENT.
SERVICES INCLUDE: VALUATIONS & FRAMING.
Please write or telephone for further exhibition details.

Puits de Leoville, St. Ouen, Jersey, Channel Islands.   Telephone: 0534-81994

LE PINACLE

Bus routes 12a
to L'Etacq
or 9a to Grosnez

In the remote north-western corner of the Island is a two hundred foot high rock which for several thousand years was the object of veneration and worship.

One of the most primitive forms of religion was the worship of holy stones (menhirs) so perhaps it is not surprising that Le Pinacle which rises steeply out of the sea close by the waterfall from a fresh-water stream, should have been chosen as a sanctified place by early man, who first came here in the Neolithic Age, around 4,500 B.C. Seven hearths and several hundred stone implements from that era have been excavated, and although no dwellings have been discovered it must be remembered that more than half the occupied site has been eroded and fallen away since those pre-historic times.

The next occupation took place between the Neolithic and Bronze Ages. Almost certainly a ceremonial site, this settlement was to the north of the first and is characterised by two earthworks and the copper artifacts, bell-beakers and barbed-and-tanged arrowheads found during excavation. During the Bronze Age and the Iron Age, man continued to come here and finally during the Roman period a temple, known as a Fanum was erected. At a time when most people had adopted the worship of Roman gods, all over Normandy, those who wanted to keep to the old religion were building similar shrines to the ancient deities. Romano-British pottery and a coin, minted in A.D. 181 and bearing the head of the Emperor Commodus were discovered here which suggests that this rectangular Gallo-Roman temple was built and used during the 3rd century A.D.

Standing at the top of the cliffs, which form a natural ampitheatre around the great rock, it is interesting to imagine those early pilgrims wending their way to this remote spot to worship the god of Le Pinacle.

It is sad to relate that in much more recent times the structures, which were restored by the Société Jersiaise, have been vandalised – sometimes through ignorance but more often by treasure-seekers using metal detectors. Readers are asked to help protect this historic site which for so many centuries was a sanctified place.

There is a tunnel cave which runs right underneath Le Pinacle. This can be reached relatively easily but should not be entered except on an out-going tide. Even then the water is always thigh-deep and there are large boulders under foot. This kind of exploration can be safe and fun as long as great care is taken, especially in relation to the state of the tide.

L'ETACQ WOODCRAFTS

Bus route 12a
Price Code E
refundable with any
purchase
Open March - November.
7 days a week.
December - February.
closed on Sundays.

This firm has been established for over thirty years and now exports to countries as far removed as Australia, Japan and the United States and has had several gift lines approved by the Design Centre in London. It has also been featured on television programmes in the U.K., on the Continent and in the United States, as well as in several national publications.

Although it has developed into a thriving tourist attraction this is not a place to see organised demonstrations in wood carving and turning: it is a commercial venture, open the whole year, where local craftsmen are working to sell – be it on a house name-board for a Jersey resident, a commission for an architect or a shut-the-box game.

Seventy types of exotic hard woods are imported from all over the world and a hundred-year-old lathe, once powered by hand, is in daily use, as are a large selection of wood turning and carving tools, so although the craftsmen are going about their business regardless of onlookers, there is plenty to see and learn.

Always of interest are the items made from the stalks of the Jersey giant cabbage – or Long Jacks. The fifteen-foot high cabbages, *Brassica oleracae longata* have been cultivated in Jersey for generations and in times past the leaves were used as food for both man and beast while the stalks were dried and used as fuel, bean-poles and tomato sticks, and for making walking sticks. Since the end of the Second World War, Phil Le Gresley, the founder of L'Etacq Woodcrafts, has been the sole manufacturer of the Jersey cabbage walking sticks – a tradition still carried on by the present craftsmen. Now several other items are also made from the stalks, including shoehorns, paperknives, keyrings and corkscrews. For those who want to grow these giants themselves there are also packets of seeds on sale in the show room.

Craftsman at work

Cabbage walking sticks

In recent times a Crafts Association has been formed in Jersey, and L'Etacq Woodcrafts has now incorporated another studio into its premises where the work of other local craftspeople is featured. Various people make use of this facility at different times: you may see a glass engraver, an artist painting on wood, someone making jewellery, or dressing Jersey dolls, or an artist painting in water-colours.

L'Etacq Woodcrafts takes commissions for work, but there is also a show-room on the premises where one can buy anything from a Jersey cabbage thimble to an ornate carving.

BATTLE OF FLOWERS MUSEUM

Bus route 9a to
Five Roads
Price Code C
Open March-October, 7 days
a week 10-5.
Winter months Tuesday and
Thursday 2-4.
Free parking
Suitable for disabled

When Florence Bechelet was ten years old, she was going low-water fishing with her grandmother when she saw a float on its way to the Battle of Flowers. She was so enchanted with what she saw that she decided there and then that she would create something similar to exhibit herself. She received no encouragement from her family, and it took longer than she had hoped, but five years later she entered her first float and won third prize. That was the start of a time-consuming but satisfying hobby that has lasted over fifty years. At first Miss Bechelet used the traditional flowers such as hydrangeas and marigolds but after three years she started entering the wild flower class and year after year she has carried off major prizes. In 1953 she began to use hare's tail and marram grasses on her floats instead of flowers; these are more easily preserved. In 1971 this museum was opened.

Dog from "The Good Old Days"

"Bevy of Beauties"

Who can say how many hare's-tails there are in the museum. In the exhibit "Good Old Days" there are 84,000 on just one horse. The themes of the floats are varied, although the creator's love of animals is obvious. A 1/9d stamp – now quite valuable – was issued bearing her 1969 design of ostriches "We're the Greatest", and in 1978 she made a special float featuring forty flamingoes called "A bevy of Beauties" to show to the Queen and the Duke of Edinburgh during their official visit to the Island.

The Battle itself started in 1902 to mark the coronation of Edward VII. It continued until the outbreak of war in 1914 and was not revived until 1928 when it moved from Victoria Avenue to Springfield. When it restarted in 1951 after World War II, Victoria Avenue was once more the venue, and it has remained there ever since. Always held on a Thursday afternoon in late July or early August it is still the high spot in the Jersey calendar – attracting thousands of spectators every year.

The actual battle, using the flowers from the floats, used to be the finale. Now things are more sedate and the floats are left intact for several days.

For those not able to attend a Battle of Flowers, it is fortunate that this museum exists and that previous exhibits such as "101 Dalmatians", "Living Free" and "Arctic Scene" can be admired – not only for their artistic merit, but also for the skill and patience of Miss Florence Bechelet who has spent hundreds of hours working on them.

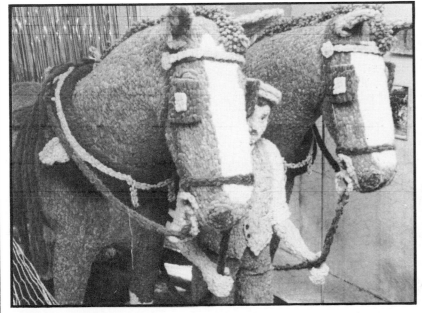

"The Good Old Days"

"101 Dalmations"

EXPLORE JERSEY WITH
Blue Coach Tours

Let us show you the beauty of the island – we will explain everything as you drive along the leafy lanes or the ever changing coastline. Our experienced drivers/guides have an intimate knowledge of the Island – not just of historical facts – but also of current affairs – information which makes our seemingly feudal world so different – not French – but not quite English.

Our fleet is modern with coaches specially built to cope with the narrow lanes – and we have a fleet of minibuses to help us provide a complete service. The weekly programme includes full day, and half day sightseeing tours, and evening drives to some of Jersey's famous Old Worlde Inns. During the season we operate daily direct trips to different beaches and to Gerald Durrell's Wildlife Preservation Trust at Les Augres Manor.

Nightlife abounds in the Island and all of the principle Cabaret venues are included in our brochure.

Tour Operators, Conference Organisers, Club Secretaries – Do you need transportation for your groups?

Please contact us for advice. We will be pleased to help you with airport/harbour transfers, special sightseeing tours or transport to sporting events at prices which might surprise you!

Telephone: (0534) 22584 or write to:
Blue Coach Tours, 70-72 Columberie, St. Helier, Jersey, for an immediate quotation.

P.S. If accommodation is a problem, contact our Travel Agency, Allen's Holidays, They may be able to help.

8 David Place, St. Helier, Jersey.
Telephone: (0534) 26248.
Telex: 4192273.

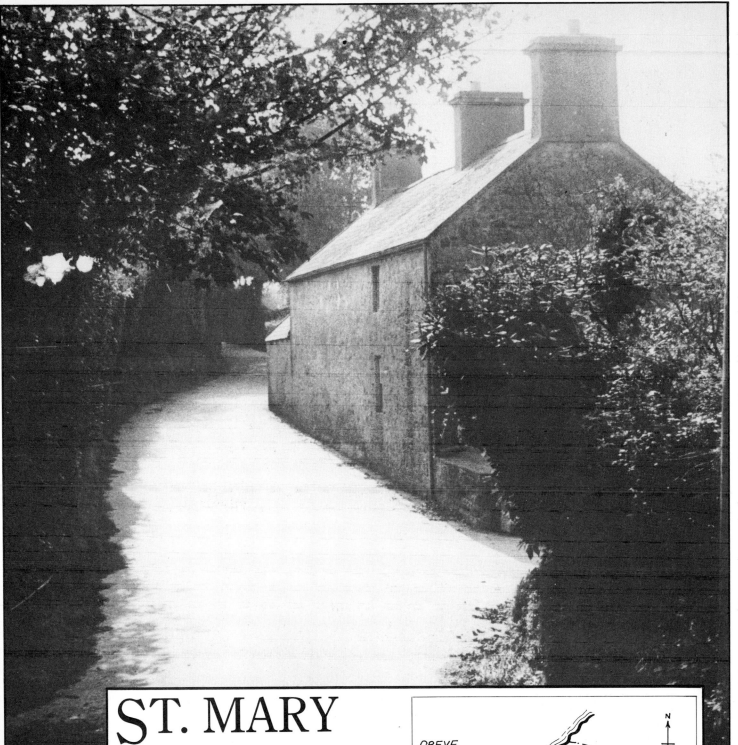

ST. MARY

This delightful parish of narrow roads and old farmhouses is the second smallest in area with only two vingtaines, and has the smallest population – 2,265 people at the last census. In the 16th and 17th centuries when knitting was a major industry, this was one of the chief sheep-breeding parishes as many field names testify.

A typical farm is The Elms, featured on the back cover of this book, which is now the working headquarters of the National Trust for Jersey. It has many unusual features and is well worth a visit by National Trust members.

The ancient church, originally called St. Mary of the Burnt Monastery, also has a fascinating history which has been well documented by local historian Joan Stevens in a short book which can be purchased at the church.

The coast-line, from Grève de Lecq to Mourier

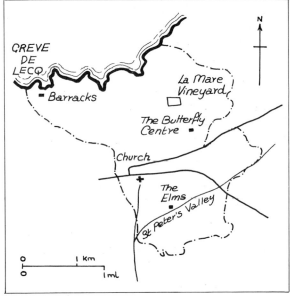

Valley, offers splendid scenery. (See coastal paths section).

GREVE DE LECQ BARRACKS

Bus route 7b, 8.
Price Code E.
Open April-October,
Monday and Thursday,
10-4.
Suitable for disabled.
National Trust shop.

It must truly have been a remote existence for the garrison troops stationed at these barracks, built at the height of the fear of a French invasion at the beginning of the 19th century.

There had, of course, been earlier defences round the bay. In 1779 the Governor of the day, General Sir Henry Seymour Conway, recommended that a Guard House be built and this was modernised in 1789 from money raised by public lottery. A tower was built in 1780 and by 1783 a redoubt had been placed on the eastern hill. A report of 1804 mentioned "two twelve-pounders on the west flank and three twelve-pounders on the east, 600 yards apart and about 100 feet above high water mark; a battery of three pounds, the foot of which is washed by spring tides; about 150 yards to the rear of this is a tower."

Old Jersey horse-drawn vehicles.

Uniforms in N.C.O. barrack room.

When they were vacated by the British Army the Barracks were used as private dwellings and then fell into disrepair. In April 1972 they were bought by the National Trust for Jersey which has restored them and now we have an excellent idea of what life must have been like.

The Barracks were designed to accommodate 150 men and one Barrack Room has been laid out to look very much as it used to with beds and uniforms. It must have been a cramped existence but at least General Don, the Governor of Jersey had the interest of his troops at heart. In 1811 he wrote two letters; one was to Captain Taylor, the Officer commanding a detatchment of the 81st Regiment stationed there and the second was to Samuel Lemprière, the Barracks Master. In the letters he insisted that the tower was not to be occupied by a guard until the walls were whitewashed. Perhaps his anxiety about the whitewashing was primarily to do with defence, but in December 1811 when Captain Taylor reported "serious deficiencies" at the Barracks, the General wrote to Lemprière again, ordering that the matter be attended to.

In one of the N.C.O.'s rooms there is a display of military equipment and records both from the Royal Jersey Militia and the British Army, and adjacent to that is a National Trust shop. The stables and harness room are at the far end.

In the third Barrack Room there is a display of old Jersey horse-drawn vehicles including a dog cart from 1875 and a very rare two-wheeled baker's delivery van which incidentally was brought back into use during the German Occupation.

No modern comforts are to be found in the ablution blocks behind the main buildings, but if those seem bleak imagine being imprisoned in the near-by prison cells . . . even for a few hours.

LA MARE VINEYARDS

Vineyards

Bus route 7, 7b.
Price Code C.
Open May-October.
Monday-Friday, 10-5.30.
Refreshments. Playground.
Shop.

The farmhouse

Wine barrels

It is not surprising that Robert Blayney, a Liveryman of the Vintners' Company whose family have been involved in the wine business since 1831, should have cherished an ambition to own his own vineyards. Why, though, did he choose Jersey – an Island that had never produced wine in any quantity?

The truth is simply that he and his wife fell in love with the Island and chose to overcome the drawbacks rather than settle in a more traditional wine-producing area.

That was in 1969 and the results speak for themselves with each year bringing greater successes. Since 1976 the Vineyards have been open to the public and now, in this most tranquil parish and on land that has belonged to the farmhouse for centuries, visitors can stroll among the vines and discover for themselves the intricacies of producing fine wine.

Vines have had to be matched to the climate and new methods adopted. Note, for example, the high trellis system, developed in New York State, that is used on the Seyval vines while, alongside, the Scheurebe variety are trained in the traditional low European fashion.

To learn the full story visit the Press House. The wine is made here in October but during the summer one can see what the owner calls "a display in praise of wine". Apart from the large press, the tanks and the casks, there are pictures, display cabinets and a short explanatory video.

If Jersey has not produced wine in the past it has certainly made plenty of cider and now La Mare is the Island's largest cider producer. In the cider house there is a display explaining the process and one can see the enormous old press which is called into action every November. It is imperative to use true cider apples to make good cider, and as local cider apple orchards are now lost, these have been grown for La Mare by a Brittany farmer.

However, in 1982 a brand new cider apple orchard was planted in the appropriately named La Pepinière (the nursery).

One can stroll in the attractive garden, enjoy a cup of tea and a home-made cake on the lawn or buy a wide variety of produce in the shop – including of course the wine and cider. Jams and mustard are made in "Uncle George's kitchen" – Uncle George having been quite a character with his secret mustard recipes and his taste for good wine.

The house itself has been faithfully restored to look very much as it did when it was built in the 18th century as a farmhouse – and of course that is what it still is. The crops have changed but it is the land that provides the living, and with no garish signs or tar-macadamed car park the atmosphere is very much that of a busy family home.

JERSEY BUTTERFLY CENTRE

A glass-house, once used for growing carnations, is the ideal venue for this "safari park for butterflies", where visitors can stroll through the main flight area among these brightly coloured insects.

The centre was opened in 1980 by Mr Arthur Rolland, whose family have been at La Haute Tombette farm for 160 years. In 1965 he built the first carnation greenhouse and opened to the public the following year. The Butterfly Centre stemmed from a concept of Mr David Lowe of Guernsey, who after starting a similar operation there, formed a partnership with Mr. Rolland.

The humid conditions in the glass-house enable tropical and sub-tropical species to breed as well as species indigenous to the British Isles which, although common a generation ago, are now becoming rarer in the wild due to pollution, weather conditions, pesticides and man's increasing demands on the environment.

P erhaps the most popular species is the Giant Atlas Moth which can be found throughout South East Asia and has a wing span of eight to ten inches. Nearly as large are the Owl butterflies of Central and South America, so named because of the large "owl eyes" on the underside of their wings. This list goes on and there are now over a hundred species reared at the Centre.

Each species needs its own special plant for food at every stage of its life cycle. This means that the main area resembles a tropical garden with nectar plants such as lantana, buddleia, honesty and milkweed growing alongside the nettles, elm and willow trees which are the breeding grounds for the European species.

Inside the enclosure

Bus route 7.
Price Code C.
Group reductions.
Open Easter-
October.

Atlas moth

Xutus butterfly

Troides Acacus

A s caterpillars have an unlimited capacity for food and would soon strip the plants, that stage is spent in special feeding areas, and these cages, along with the cages protecting the pupae during the chrysalis stage are set within the main area.

H ow long a butterfly lives depends on the species, but here one can follow every stage in its life cycle: the mating and egg-laying; the egg hatching into larva and the caterpillar spinning its cocoon. If you are lucky, you may witness the small miracle of a butterfly emerging, unfolding its wings and flying for the first time.

ST. JOHN

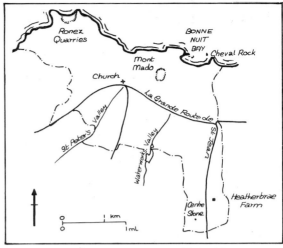

Another northern parish with a fine coast-line described in the Coastal Walks section of this book, St. John is also famous for its granite quarries: Ronez which is still worked, and Mont Mado from where the finest pink granite has been extracted from as far back as prehistoric times.

St. John has a fine Recreation Centre which includes the £250,000 extension, the Sir Billy Butlin Memorial Hall, opened by His Royal Highness the Duke Edinburgh in 1983. Sir Billy was a resident of St. John and is buried in the parish church cemetery.

The centre of the Island lies within the parish and is marked by a stone in the garden of Centre House just north of Sion Methodist Church. On the other side of the main road can be seen the cemetery of Macpéla where many of the European exiles who sought refuge in Jersey in the mid-nineteenth century were buried with great ceremony. On these occasions the whole exiled colony used to march to the cemetery behind the Red Flag and fiery orations were delivered, often by that most famous of French exiles – Victor Hugo.

Horse riding down le Neuf Chemin

BONNE NUIT BAY

There are many stories as to how the bay got its name: it first appears in the 12th century when Guillaume de Vauville gave the Chapel of Ste. Marie in St. John's Parish to the Abbey of St. Saveur le Vicomte. The King, when confirming the gift, called it the Chapel of Bonne Nuit (de Bono Nocte). Shortly afterwards, when Guillaume's son Richard was selling a field he described it as "alongside the Chapel de Mala Nocte" which is a bit confusing but perhaps the solution is in the fact that for centuries the sea outside the bay was called Maurepos (ill repose) and it could therefore be assumed that a "Good Night" was had if a boat reached the shore. Alternatively the name change could have been an insurance against bad luck.

There is a rock in the middle of the bay called Le Cheval Guillaume, and on Midsummer Day – which is also St. John's Day – people from all over the Island used to flock to Bonne Nuit to be rowed round the rock. This was to avoid bad luck and is an ancient custom dating back to pagan times. In 1792 Philippe Dumaresq, who founded Jersey's first newspaper, decided to liven up the proceedings and instituted a two-day fair with an open-air market, an ox-roasting, entertainments such as comedians and tight-rope dancers from France, and a fire-work display. Unfortunately after five years the States suppressed the whole event as being "contrary to good morals".

Like other vulnerable spots round the coast, Bonne Nuit was considered a possible landing-place for an enemy, so it has had its share of defences. A boulevard for two cannons was erected in 1736, then a guard house was built followed by a powder magazine. La Crête Fort at the eastern extremity of the bay was built in 1835, and is now put at the disposal of the Lieutenant-Governor. Lastly a barracks was built on the site where the Cheval Roc Hotel stands now – but no attack materialised. Instead the bay was used extensively by smugglers and at least one house in the area is known to have been built from the proceeds of such activities.

La Vallette
Bus route 5.

Bonne Nuit Bay looking east

The 400 foot high cliffs surrounding the bay afford shelter, and bathing is good at high tide. The view from Frémont Point to the west of the bay, is spectacular, and well worth the short climb.

The National Trust for Jersey owns the land on both sides of the road leading eastwards from Bonne Nuit Bay and in 1977 the Trust, together with members of the National Conservation Corps, cut a circular path into the hillside on the landward side. This makes a pleasant walk and again the views are breathtaking. The National Trust also owns the farmhouse of La Vallette at the top of the hill which, in its present form, was built in 1796. The property is let and may only be visited by arrangement between the tenant and the Council of the Trust.

La Crête Fort

HEATHERBRAE FARM

When, in 1982, Hugh and Chris Taylor opened their 40-acre dairy farm to the public for an experimental ten weeks, they had no idea how popular it would prove. Many people have never been on a farm, while others have not had the chance to see cows milked or calves fed, nor had explained to them the statistical data it is necessary to keep on a modern farm.

The Jersey cow, with her large eyes fringed with long lashes, her mealy muzzle and her fine coat, is famous throughout the world: even people who have never been to Jersey are familiar with her and the reputation she has for producing rich creamy milk.

In 1830, however, she was far from her present perfection, even though earlier legislation had banned the importation of cattle to the Island. A Colonel Le Couteur described the Jersey as "The Meg Merrilies of the bovine race", and it was largely due to his energy and foresight that in 1833 the Jersey (now Royal Jersey) Agricultural and Horticultural Society was founded and farmers set about breeding the compact, well-proportioned animal that is so famous today. The value of the Jersey's rich milk has gained world-wide recognition, but that is not the only reason why breeders from all over the world buy Jersey cattle. Despite her delicate appearance, the Jersey has an astonishing ability to withstand extremes of climate with no ill effect and has a natural immunity to many diseases.

Heatherbrae Farm was started in 1980, aiming to produce a good yield and butterfat content from a herd of 40 milking cows. The yield per cow is

Coming in from fields for milking

Bus route 5
Price Code C
Open May –
September
Monday-Saturday
2.30 – 5.30
Guided tours
Teas
Playground

Milking parlour

currently about 880 gallons a year at around six per cent butterfat, and only the heifers from the higher yielding cows are kept. The farm also keeps two bulls for breeding.

The herd cannot survive on grass alone, so crops are also grown: four acres of barley to produce straw for bedding and grain which is rolled and fed to young stock; two acres of maize for autumn feeding and two acres of kale for winter feeding. The 32 acres of grass not only feed the herd in the summer but produces 4,000 bales of hay for winter feeding.

As with all milk produced locally, that from Heatherbrae is sent to the Jersey Milk dairy at Five Oaks for Island use. About 76 per cent is sold in liquid form and the rest is manufactured into cream, yoghurt and butter. Now the high quality of milk is maintained through weekly checks on all milk coming into the dairy, and the laboratory at Five Oaks is one of the most modern in the British Isles.

The Island is proud of its long tradition of selective breeding in cattle and is striving to maintain it. At Heatherbrae the visitor can begin to appreciate the reason why.

TRINITY

This large and relatively unpopulated parish is full of interesting places: the remains of a vast earthwork on Les Cateaux, a farm to the south of the Jersey Wildlife Preservation Trust for example, where in 1406 thousands of people sought refuge when Hector de Pontbriand and Pero Niño invaded the Island. On being told that they would have to kill every man, woman and child before they would be allowed to enter this "ville", the raiders accepted a ransom and sailed away.

The Parish church possesses the oldest piece of silverware in the Island, a pre-Reformation chalice. There is also a fine mural monument to Sir Edouard de Carteret, Black Rod under Charles II, who was buried here in 1683 because the horses drawing the hearse to his funeral at St. Ouen's bolted and stopped only when they arrived at the gate of this, his parish church.

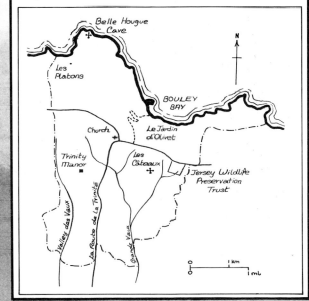

Mist covering field at Ville à l'Eveque

LES PLATONS AND LA BELLE HOUGUE

Climb down to Belle Hougue cave

Bus route 4 to Le Vesconte Monument

Author being shown entrance to cave

For those who enjoy climbing cliffs and exploring caves, mention should be made of the cave at La Belle Hougue, although it must be stressed that only fit people armed with plenty of rope, torches and preferably a local guide should attempt this.

Approaching from La Rue d'Egypte one sees Les Platons on the left. This area is the highest point in the Island (149 metres) and the masts of Rediffusion (Jersey) Ltd., the B.B.C. Television and Decca Navigator Radio Transmitting Station are all situated there. Also on Les Platons (found by taking the track to the north-west of Les Platons Road) is a late Bronze Age burial mound known as La Hougue des Platons where two urns, one containing the cremated remains of a woman and child, were found, and can be seen in the Archaeological Museum at La Hougue Bie.

However – back to our climb. Having gone down La rue d'Egypte continue straight on, down the grass track which eventually turns left. Straight ahead is La Fontaine és Mittes – a mineral spring which was once said to have "the miraculous power of loosening the tongue and giving speech to the dumb" as well as curing eye complaints. The path then leads towards the cliffs and shortly small concrete posts can be found on which to secure the first set of ropes. (However as these are quite old, it is as well to utilise nearby boulders as well!). Having scrambled down the cliffs aided by the ropes, veer to the left and below can be found the easiest entrance to the cave. Again, ropes are absolutely necessary, but down that narrow entrance is a cave 33 yards long. This had long been hidden by an ancient rock fall but was discovered by students in 1914 when it contained many large stalactites and stalagmites. Antlers, teeth and bones of a small prehistoric deer unknown elsewhere (which has been named *Cervus elephus jerseyensis*) were also found as were quantities of sea gravel containing shells – some only found in warmer water. No human remains were discovered and these animal relics have been dated to approximately 120,000 B.C.

Exploring inside cave

Sadly, many of the stalactites and stalagmites have been removed but, with the aid of torches, it is possible to see new ones forming. At the back of the cave, on a higher level, there is still the sea-gravel containing shells and below is a small fresh water pond – probably with the same healing powers as the spring above!

Fish and crabs can be found at the other end of the cave where the sea seeps through, apparently leading a healthy and protected – if somewhat dark – existence.

Unlike the fish, humans hopefully grow no larger while inside the cave, so it is possible to emerge through the narrow entrance and climb back up the cliff. La Belle Hougue is well-named – the view from the top is indeed beautiful and is well appreciated at the end of the climb.

Holidays in one of Jersey's Seymour Hotels are rather special.

Surfing in St. Brelade's Bay, overlooked by the Portelet Hotel

Dining in elegance at the Portelet Hotel

Cocktail hour at the Pomme d'Or Hotel

You'll discover just how memorable a holiday in Jersey can be if you choose one of the premier Seymour Hotels of Jersey. Situated at the sea's edge, the luxurious Hotel de la Plage offers gracious comfort and 4-Star service. The Portelet Hotel overlooking the sweep of St. Brelade's Bay offers outstanding facilities including a sun-trap pool, tennis court and extensive gardens. Overlooking the St. Helier Marina, the Pomme d'Or is right at the heart of the town with many facilities for non-residents — the Tavern Carvery, the Wunderbar Bierkeller and the Le Pommier Coffee Shop.

HOTEL DE LA PLAGE AA & RAC**** 1st Reg. ████
Havre des Pas, St. Helier, Jersey. Tel. 23474

PORTELET HOTEL AA**** 1st Reg. ████
Portelet Bay, St. Brelade, Jersey. Tel. 41204

POMME D'OR HOTEL AA & RAC **** 1st Reg. ████
Esplanade, St. Helier, Jersey. Tel. 78644

Seymour Hotels of Jersey

FINEST VALUE IN THE CHANNEL ISLES

Call at any of the Seymour Hotels or telephone or write to
SEYMOURS LTD.,
1 Wharf Street,
St. Helier, Jersey.
Tel. 78644 (STD 0534)

BOULEY BAY

Set between high cliffs and reached by a steep, winding road, this bay is sheltered and beautiful at all times of the year. For those interested in geology, the beach is one of the best areas in Jersey to see volcanic rock. The multi-coloured pebbles, formed by lava, ashes and a mixture of rock cemented together date back seven hundred million years to the time when great volcanoes emerged and spread hot ash and lava over a wide area.

Bouley Bay

Bus route 4

Bouley Bay is also a good place for skin diving, but the inexperienced swimmer should not venture into the sea here as the shingle shelves rapidly. The water in the bay is very deep and in the nineteenth century it was proposed to build a large harbour here. This never came about, probably because the steep hills would have caused too many problems, but at least there would have been no chance of silting, as was the case with St. Catherine's. As it is, Bouley has just a small pier, built in 1827, although the bay has had its moments of excitement. In 1547 for example, an expedition from France seized Sark, and after failing to take Guernsey, landed in Bouley Bay and fought the Militia at Jardin d'Olivet, the common land nearly 500 feet up on the eastern cliff-top. In the ensuing battle the Lieutenant-Bailiff of Jersey was killed but the French were routed and returned to St. Malo with their dead and wounded.

Due to its position Bouley Bay has always been vulnerable to attack and so from the earliest times it has been fortified. One of the first cannons in the island was placed here and two bulwarks were built as well as a guard-house, magazines and a beacon. The remains of Leicester Battery and Les Hurets Magazine can be seen on the west of the bay and L'Etacquerel Fort, built between 1786 and 1790 is situated to the east.

There are two legends about Bouley Bay. One concerns a black dog, as big as a man, with eyes like saucers, who is supposed to roam the cliff paths at night. Some say it is a warning of an approaching storm, others that it was a story put about by smugglers to keep people away from the area but whatever the origin of the black dog, he has never been known to harm anybody. The other legend

Skin diving school

dates back to the French occupation of Jersey in the 15th century when bands of French sheep-thieves would roam the northern parishes. A young Jersey girl, whose fiancé was killed by these brigands, leapt to her death from Les Tombelènes, the cliffs to the east, to L'Islet, the rock in the bay. Ever since her cry, the cry of the Tombelènes, is said to be heard on certain winter nights.

These days Bouley Bay is known for happier events – the hill climbs. The Jersey Motor Cycle and Light Car Club have been organising these since the 1930s and they now hold three a year: on Easter and Spring Bank holiday Mondays there are Club events and in July a round of the British Hill Climb Championship is held. The length of the timed section is 1,011 yards and at the time of going to press the all-out record, created in 1981 by Martin Bolsover, is 39 seconds dead. There are classes for motorcycles, karts, saloon cars, racing cars and sports cars, and events for cycles and karts are also held annually. Parking is free. Price Code C. Children free.

Le Jardin d'Olivet (La Commune du fief de la Gruchetterie) and the adjoining common (La Commune du fief de Dièlament) can be reached by a footpath from the beach and are popular for picnics and walks. Note the Victorian gazebo in the

north-west corner. It must have been a delightful retreat in the last century before the trees obscured the view of the bay below.

Another pleasant walk in the area is through the National Trust property La Grand Côtil du Boulay. From the bay, walk up the hill until the junction with a road with a "No entry" sign. Just past this, on the right of the main road is the entrance to the walk, which goes up the côtil, passing a pond on the right. At the top is Lé Puchot (which means a water course in the form of a pond). Here the stream runs through an enclosure containing a lavoir and alongside is a wellhead fronted by a wrought iron gate. The path to the left of Lé Puchot brings one to Rue de la Petite Falaise. Straight ahead is another National Trust property known as Le Don Le Breton, which is a strip of land which formed part of the field opposite until the road was built. These strips are known as 'issues' and this one is planted with trees and shrubs including hydrangeas and giant fuschia bushes.

Turning left to return to the top of Bouley Bay Hill, one passes the Common of the Fief de l'Abbesse de Caen – a name dating back to the days when the French religious orders owned a lot of Jersey land. This is another area where one can picnic, admire the view or make one's way back down towards the bay.

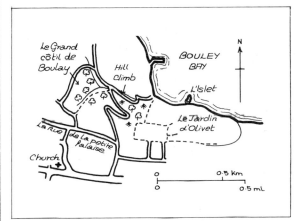

Gazebo at Jardin d'Olivet

Bouley Bay in Victorian times

83

THE JERSEY WILDLIFE PRESERVATION TRUST

Founded in 1959 by the zoologist and best-selling author Gerald Durrell, and created as a Trust four years later, this is a unique place where over 1,200 of the world's rarest animals are able to breed in peace, free from predators, with an unfailing food supply, the finest veterinary attention and with the best possible accommodation.

Perhaps the most popular resident is Jambo, the patriarch of Jersey's lowland gorilla family and the father of more offspring than any other captive male gorilla. His spacious home which he shares with his wives and their progeny has been carefully designed to add to the quality of their lives. Opened in 1981 the complex consists of a large house with enough room for the whole family to play, eat, sleep or be alone, and half an acre of undulating ground outside with climbing frames, boulders and natural vegetation. With that sort of environment, it is no wonder that the animals are contented and that the Trust is one of the most successful zoos in the world in breeding this threatened species.

In terms of popularity, the other species of great ape – the orang-utan – is high on the list. They too are reproducing successfully which is good news, for we are told they could disappear from the wild by the end of the century.

"Given the money I could build the best reptile house in the world!" So said Gerald Durrell to a Canadian back in the early 70s. Little did he know that he was talking to a millionaire with a life-long interest in reptiles and that the result of that comment would be the Gaherty Reptile Breeding Centre, opened by the Trust's patron, H.R.H. Princess Anne in October 1976. Now, many rare species of reptile are breeding successfully in spacious units and visitors are able to see some of the results in a group of nursery cages erected in the exhibition hall.

Everyone has their own particular favourites, be they the lemurs from Madagascar, the exotic marmosets and the tamarins from South America, the snow leopards from Central Asia or the cheetahs and serval cats from the African continent. The list goes on, and it would be impossible to mention all the inhabitants of Gerald Durrell's "Menagerie Manor", but two more not to be missed are the spectacled bear from South America and the only true wild horse in existence – the Przewalski's horse.

Cheetahs

Bus route 3a, 3b.
Price Code A.
Open all year, 10-6pm.
Café.
Gift shop.
Suitable for disabled.
Guide Book.

Lowland gorillas

And then there are the infinite variety of birds from parrots and pheasants to the tiny but colourful Rodrigues fody. One of Jersey's greatest success stories is with the Mauritius pink pigeon — one of the rarest birds in the world with an estimated wild population of fifteen. So successful has the breeding programme here been that birds have been sent back to Mauritius — and some have now been released back into the wild, and are surviving.

Gerald Durrell and friend – a Scarlet Macaw (Philip Coffey – Jersey Wildlife Preservation Trust)

Wallaby

Give yourself enough time to see everything and to enjoy the surroundings – the old manor surrounded by a 16th century walled courtyard, the twenty acres of landscaped park land and the natural lakes. Where better to have a picnic than on the grass overlooking the lakes, watching the graceful pink Chilean flamingoes.

This then is all that a zoo should be – but is it a zoo? Had it been called a breeding centre for endangered species many people might stay away, but that is exactly what it is. The Jersey Wildlife Preservation Trust was founded to build up breeding colonies of various species of animals threatened with extinction in the wild state. Happily several other zoos have now followed its example but the Trust is still unique in that it sends key members of its staff to different parts of the world to study, in the wild state, the animals in their care.

It also runs a Training Centre for people from those countries so that they can carry out their own captive breeding programmes.

The purpose of the Trust, therefore, is not to provide entertainment for us but to create a sanctuary for endangered species. That is the secret of its success, for no-one really wants to see miserable animals eeking out a lonely existence behind bars. How much more rewarding and exciting it is to know that just by visiting this zoo we are enabling the Trust to carry out their vitally important work of conservation. After all – who wants to live in a world with no wildlife?

Gorilla Complex   Mauritius Pink Pigeon

ST. MARTIN

The parish of St. Martin has a very long coast-line for its size with no less than seven bays and numerous creeks and coves. It is also the most wooded parish in the island, having several sheltered valleys. It is a rural parish with three village communities, that of St. Martin which is centred round the church, and Rozel and Gorey which grew around the fishing trade. Both Rozel and Gorey are divided between two parishes – part of Rozel is in Trinity and while the pier and castle at Gorey are in St. Martin, most of the village is in Grouville.

The Seigneurial manor of Rosel is not open to the public. On certain occasions, however, the grounds are made available for special events and at those times a visit is recommended. The gardens are beautifully laid out and spring-flowering shrubs and trees offer a marvellous setting for the chapel, built well before 1461.

The Ecréhous reef is part of St Martin's parish. There are three main islands in the reef – Maître Ile, Marmotière and Blanche Ile. In 1953 the International Court of Justice at The Hague upheld

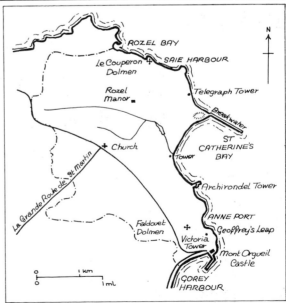

Britain's claim of sovereignty over the Ecréhous and the Minquiers.

Le Couperon

The castles of Jersey

Mount Orgueil Castle, Gorey Tel: 53292

MONT ORGUEIL

"A medieval concentric castle of unique beauty and strength." Open daily from 9.30 a.m. to 6 p.m. Last admission 5.30 p.m. including Sundays. Admission includes entry to the tableaux which, with a commentary, tells the story of the Castle.

Elizabeth Castle

"A Truly massive fortress" in St. Aubin's Bay. Open daily from 9.30 a.m. to 6 p.m. Last admission 5.30 p.m. including Sundays. Admission includes entry to the tableaux and militia museum. A private D.U.K.W. service operates to the Castle, weather permitting.

Elizabeth Castle, St Aubin's Bay   Tel: 23971

Full cafeteria facilities are available at both castles.

ROZEL

Rozel Harbour showing viviers for fish

Bus route 3

Rozel Bay at the turn of the century (G. Amy)

Old barracks, now Le Couperon de Rozel Hotel from beach

Rozel harbour, built in 1829 at the peak of the oyster trade is in Trinity, although most of the village is in St. Martin. A Victorian naturalist describes Rozel as "one of the most attractive" bays and continues, "it is a Voe or deep creek rather than a bay. Deep and shady glens wooded with various trees lead from it into the interior, while its sides are rugged and precipitous and echo the sound of the long roll of the waves upon the beach. The descent to it is by tortuous path and near the sea are scattered the cottages of a few fishermen. Some untenanted barracks are also to be seen near the spot". These barracks, seemingly unused in 1850 were built in 1809 when Jersey was thought to be in danger of a French invasion. They are now part of Le Couperon Hotel.

Rozel has now become very popular and so is not quite the peaceful place it was in the last century, but the beach is ideal for children, the small boats in the harbour make an attractive sight and all the amenities are readily available.

For those wishing to explore there is a pleasant walk through Rozel Valley. From the harbour turn right and then left past some of the original fishermen's cottages and Le Couperon Hotel and then turn right again. Samuel William Curtis, editor of the Botanical Magazine, lived in this valley in the early nineteenth century and planted many trees and shrubs which can still be enjoyed today. Perhaps the most famous and beautiful is the giant Himalaya pink tulip tree *magnolia campbellii* which flowers in the early spring. This species was not introduced into Europe until 1870, by which time Curtis had died, so this particular tree may well have been planted by his daughter. Flowering later, in May and June is the Davidia *involucrata* or handkerchief tree, so named because its flowers resemble handkerchiefs hanging from the branches.

Just after the road turns to the left there is an old fountain set in the wall below Camellia Cottage, and further along there are rows of willows grown for basket-making. At the top of the hill, now set in private property is Rozel Mill, one of the most ancient windmills in Jersey. It was shown as one of only three windmills in the island on Popinjay's map of 1563 and the walls are very thick. In bygone years it has belonged to famous families, such as the Bandinels and the Lemprières. In 1920 it was acquired by the Harbours Committee as a landmark and during the Occupation it was adapted and used by the Germans as an observation post.

166 JERSEY. — Le Moulin de Rozel. — Rozel Mill. — LL.

Rozel Mill at the turn of the century (R.H. Mayne)

PERQUAGE PATH
(walk through Rozel Woods)

Bus routes 3, 3a

The perquage path from St. Martin's church runs through Rozel Woods to the coast south of St. Catherine's. Imagine, if you like, that you are a pre-Reformation criminal and this is your only route to freedom. The path can get muddy, though, so go prepared. Allow 1½ hours for the full circuit of the walk.

From the east of the church, walk a short way down La Grande Route de Rozel, and turn right into La Rue des Vaux de l'Eglise. A little way down you will see a fine example of a lavoir and abreuvoir inscribed with the sets of initials of the people authorised to use it. Above this can be seen Bandinel Farm, built in 1619. David Bandinel, Dean of Jersey at the time of the Civil War, lived here. He was imprisoned in Mont Orgueil Castle because he supported the anti-royalists, and died from injuries sustained when he tried to escape in 1645.

At the bottom of the hill turn left into a meadow and follow the path by the stream. This next area can get extremely muddy but before long you arrive at a T-junction. Here the stream joins another from the west, so turn right and follow its route. Flag irises grow abundantly in this valley and it is one of the few places in Jersey where yellow archangel, dog's mercury, climbing white fumitory and wood sorrel can be found. The greater spotted woodpecker is known to breed in these woods, and red squirrels can often be seen in the trees.

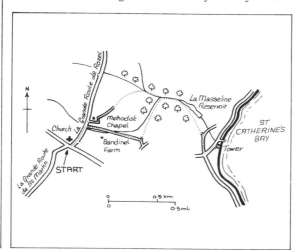

Stepping stones across stream

La Masseline Reservoir

The stream is crossed twice by stepping stones and then La Masseline Reservoir is reached. This was built by the Germans and is a popular venue for members of the Jersey Fresh Water Angling Association for coarse and trout fishing.

Around another bend and the sea is visible. Those who want to follow the perquage path to its natural conclusion should take the main road and head for the round tower, built between 1779 and 1801 and now used as a marker for shipping. To the north is St. Catherine's and to the south is a stretch of road known as Pine Walk, leading to Archirondel. For the return it is possible to take an alternative route. Past the reservoir and the first set of stepping-stones take the right hand fork which takes you above the stream until a wooden bridge is crossed on to the original path beside the meadow. This time, do not take the muddy path to the left but keep straight on until another T-junction is reached. This is Rue des Mares and a nineteenth century map shows that it was once a road. The track to the right is a possible walk to St. Catherine's. Note the drinking area built into the bridge, but take the left hand track. This is a gentle climb with good views of the valley below. The track eventually becomes a road which leads past St. Martin's Methodist Church into La Grande Route de Rozel. Before turning left to the church, walk about sixty yards to the right to see the oldest working forge in the island. The church is well worth a visit either before or after the walk.

ST CATHERINE'S BAY

Bus route 2.

Archirondel and Havre de Fer from La Crette Point

Historically very little happened in this bay until the mid-nineteenth century. True, a pirate was hanged here in 1500 and in common with other exposed coastlines, defensive towers were built towards the end of the eighteenth century. One at Fliquet generally referred to as the Telegraph Tower, St. Catherine's Tower and Archirondel Tower, which later had a platform added which formed the pattern for La Rocco Tower in St. Ouen's Bay.

It was the 1840s, though, that saw the start of great activity in the area. The British Government, worried at the extensive improvements the French were making to their own ports from Brest to Dunkirk, and especially at Cherbourg, decided to build four so-called "Harbours of Refuge" at Harwich, Dover, Alderney and Jersey. That at St. Catherine's was intended to be a stepping off point for an invasion of the Cotentin and was to have one arm from Archirondel and the other from Verclut. Although the Admiralty were warned by Admiral Martin White, an authority on local waters, that the proposed harbour would quickly silt up, work commenced on both arms on 30th June 1847. A steam tramway was built to transport the stone and it was then that the last remaining wall of the chapel of St. Catherine was demolished, revealing the skeletons of five members of the religious fraternity buried nearby.

Work on the Archirondel arm was abandoned on 31st July 1849, but the Verclut breakwater, which is 2,300 feet long, took nine years to complete. The actual cost was £234,235 16s. 0d, but as the Government also purchased large tracts of land and properties the total lay-out was over £300,000. The euphemistic name "Harbour of Refuge" was intended to hoodwink the French, which it never did, but finally the whole venture was abandoned: partly because of the Entente Cordiale with France, but more particularly because it was useless. It lacked sufficient depth of water and could never have been made to work. "What a series of blunders these Admiralty Harbours have been" quoted a gentleman in the Board of Trade in 1866.

On 23rd February 1876 the breakwater was transferred free of charge to the States of Jersey, who accepted it with reluctance. Luckily it had been well built, and has needed very little upkeep, unlike the similar project in Alderney which has proved to be in constant need of repair.

During the Occupation of World War II a gun emplacement was built into the rock opposite the breakwater, which has since proved an ideal place to keep shell-fish, and is now used as a commercial 'vivier'.

St. Catherine's breakwater

2nd world war gun emplacement – now a vivier

The flat damp areas on the inland side of the road, just after it divides to go round the large rock, contain grass poly (*lythrum hyssopifolia*) a plant extremely rare in the British Isles and not found elsewhere in the Channel Islands.

Nineteenth century British taxpayers may have suffered financially from the building of St. Catherine's Breakwater, but these days yachtsmen, anglers and families using the facility of special barbecue areas or merely out for a stroll do not regret too deeply the "monumental blunder" of the British Admiralty.

MONT ORGUEIL CASTLE

Mont Orgueil, or Gorey Castle, is without doubt the most famous and photographed place in Jersey. Its strategic position on a rock within sight of France indicates that there were fortifications here long before the castle was built, and proof of at least one Iron Age earthwork can be seen in the Middle Ward of the castle.

Mont Orgueil

View of Grouville Bay from top of castle

Bus routes 1, 1a, 2
Price Code C
Open 9.30-5.30
Tearoom
Guide Book

The present castle dates from the time when King John lost Normandy in 1204. France suddenly became enemy territory and defence became the chief priority of de Suligny, the Warden of Jersey at the time, who built a small fort on the site. The Keep on the edge of the cliff was de Suligny's work, and this was probably surrounded by an outer wall. Over the next few years raids on the island were frequent, but the castle was added to and strengthened and usually withstood the attacks. Strangely it was the Wars of the Roses which caused the most successful raid. Marguerite of Anjou, wife of Henry VI, was a staunch Lancastrian and in 1461 her cousin, Pierre de Brézé, Compte de Moulevrier, attacked Jersey presumably to help her declining cause. His cousin Jean de Carbonnel led a force which surprised the castle and went on to conquer the rest of the Island. So started a cruel and oppressive occupation which lasted seven years. Leading Jerseymen disappeared without trace and farmers lived in fear of their sheep being stolen by bands of brigands known as Les Moutonniers. It was at this time that the castle became known as Mont Orgueil (Mount Pride). Some say it was a compliment paid by the brother of Henry V, but it could have referred to the arrogant pride of the occupation force or it may even have been the invention of some romantic French exile. Eventually in 1468, Sir Richard Harliston, under the Yorkist King Edward IV, besieged and regained the castle. He built the tower over the first gateway which still bears his name.

In the late 16th century, with the ever-increasing range of cannon-fire, Mont Orgueil became much more vulnerable to attack. Three generations of the Poulet family had been governors of the Island, spending tremendous sums on Mont Orgueil, but in 1593 Anthony Poulet, whose arms can still be seen over the fourth gateway, decided that this money had been wasted. The Council of State had reported "The Castle lieth subject to a mighty hill but 400 feet distant and so overtopt by it that no man can possibly show his face in defence this side next this hill". And so it was decided to build a new castle on L'Islet, the island commanding the entrance to St. Helier, the legislative capital of the Island. When Sir Anthony Poulet died in 1600 Sir Walter Raleigh became Governor, and it was due to him that the castle was not destroyed. He wrote to Lord Cecil that "it is a stately fort of great capacity . . . it were a pity to cast it down having cost her Majesty's father, brother and sister – without her own charge – 20,000 marks in the erecting".

The Cornish Bastion

Tableau showing Admiral Philippe d'Auvergne

Tableau of the Paulet family

The Queen Victoria Gate

Prisoners were still kept in the castle, which caused a good deal of inconvenience to the halberdiers, king's tenants who lived in St. Martin, Grouville and St. Saviour, whose tenure obliged them to march the prisoners to and from the Court in St. Helier. One famous political prisoner was William Prynne, the Puritan writer and pamphleteer who, because he had tried to reform the morals of the age, had twice had his ears cropped and had S. L. (seditious libeller) branded on both cheeks.

While the Civil War raged, Mont Orgueil again increased in importance. Anne Dowse, the wife of the Governer, Sir Philippe de Carteret, bravely held it for the King while her husband defended Elizabeth Castle, and it stayed a Royalist stronghold until 1651 when, without a battle, the Commonwealth troops under Colonel James Heane were handed the keys by troops completely demoralised by the outcome of the Battle of Worcester. During these troubled years political prisoners from both sides were incarcerated in the dungeons, some losing their lives, but with the Restoration and the subsequent building of the town prison in 1693 Mont Orgueil returned to a peaceful existence.

The next major excitement was during the French Revolution when, for about eight years a pro-Royalist secret service known as "La Correspondance" operated from the castle. Admiral Philippe d'Auvergne, who commanded the Jersey Naval Station and who lived at the castle, ran an underground movement into France and passed valuable information on to London. He was also responsible for thousands of French refugees and entertained many of the French nobility in great style at the castle.

For the next hundred years, its useful life over, Mont Orgueil fell into disrepair, but in 1907 the Crown handed it over to the States and visitors were allowed in. During the Occupation it was once more a military fortress – its walls were strengthened with concrete and look out posts and fire-control points were installed on the summit. Even roll-bombs were suspended from the walls in case of attack.

St. George's Crypt

Today the castle enjoys serene old age. Visitors have plenty to explore: there are tableaux depicting its most historic events, the wall lizard (*lacerta muralis*) can be seen in great numbers on its walls and the view from its ramparts is magnificent. Look carefully towards France. It is said that on a clear day it is possible to see the spires of Coutances Cathedral.

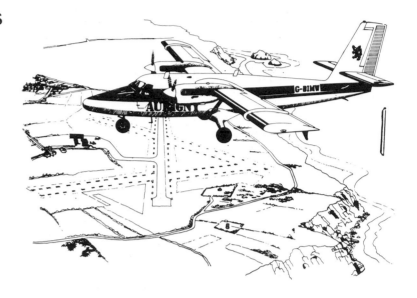
STATES OF JERSEY

1983 saw the first major design change in 140 years of Jersey coinage. Instead of the Seal of the Bailiwick being depicted on the reverse, each denomination now has an individual design depicting a local landmark symbolic of one of six periods of the Island's history. The 1983 one pound coin is the first of a series of twelve to be issued twice yearly showing the Parish emblems.

Limited issues of sterling silver and 22 carat gold together with specially selected uncirculated coins in presentation packs are available from recognised outlets throughout the Island.

For full details please write to:

THE COIN ADVISER, STATES TREASURY, JERSEY, C.I.
Please send me details of:

☐ Current & Future Coin Issues ☐ Previous Coin Issues

☐ Jersey Banknotes ☐ Mintage Figures

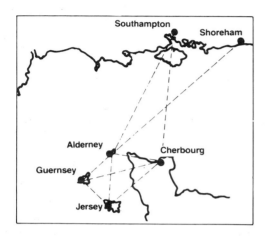

Name (Mr/Mrs/Miss) ....
(Please Print)

Address ....

....

We can now offer Barclaycard and Access facilities

LE COUPERON DOLMEN AND SAIE HARBOUR

Bus route 3, 3b to top of Rozel Hill.

The gallery grave of Le Couperon is worth visiting, if only to admire its setting just above Saie Harbour.

The B 91 road down to the harbour is very steep, narrow and winding, and can get congested during the summer, but an alternative way to reach the area is to walk from the top of Rozel Hill, just before the Bistro Frère restaurant. This path, known as Les Fontenelles winds into the valley past cultivated côtils and has lovely views of the secluded inlet Douet de la Mer. Wild flowers are plentiful and include snowdrops, violets, pennywort and bluebells, while the headland beyond the dolmen is covered with Jersey thrift and sea campions and daffodils. Saie Harbour itself is one of the best places to examine the strange formation of Rozel Conglomerate, the 'pudding-mix' rock peculiar to the area. The grave itself was inaccurately restored in 1868 and again adjusted in 1919. There are only two known gallery graves in Jersey, the other being in First Tower Park, St. Helier. They probably evolved from the earlier passage graves around 2,000 B.C. and were essentially parallel sided cists covered by a mound used for collective burial. Elsewhere some gallery graves have a port-hole formed by two upright stones, each with a cut-out semi-circle. There is one such stone at the east end of Le Couperon. It is clearly in the wrong position, and its partner is missing. In the original 'restoration' it was used as a capstone, but was moved to its present position in 1919.

Le Pouquelaye de Faldouet: Bus route 1, 1a to Gorey and then walk up the hill

La Coupe Point to the east of Le Saie, can be reached across the beach if the tide is out, otherwise it can be approached from the road. Braye Rock beyond the point is the most easterly tip of Jersey (except for St. Catherine's Breakwater) and cowrie shells can usually be discovered on the shore-line.

LA POUQUELAYE DE FALDOUET

This Neolithic dolmen, approached through an avenue of trees from Rue des Marettes, has been so changed by would-be archaeological diggers and restorers over the centuries that it is impossible to say for certain how it looked originally. A passage of 17 stones leads to a roughly circular chamber surrounded by the remains of side-cells, and beyond that is a horseshoe chamber of seven uprights covered by a huge capstone weighing about 24 tons. Because of its size, this is perhaps the only part of the monument not to suffer from early 'restoration' but it was certainly exposed in the 17th century when it was recorded that a man could creep under it. Present-day experts think that it is possible that this chamber and the passage originally formed a straightforward passage-grave, and that the western end of the passage was later dug out to form a second grave. Several human remains were found, including children's bones. One skeleton is said to have been in a sitting position, similar to that found at Monts Grantez. The human remains were reburied and unfortunately the precise points of discovery of the pottery, stone-axes and flints were not recorded, so it is impossible to test the two-period theory.

Le Couperon Dolmen

95

First choice in Jersey!

If you appreciate old world charm coupled with modern luxury then you'll soon fall under the spell of La Place Hotel. The heart of the hotel is an old farmhouse – circa 1640, the low ceilings, blackened beams and huge open hearth provide an atmosphere of warmth and well being. All bedrooms have modern facilities, some with access onto the swimming pool patio. The quality of the food and service is of the highest standard – always associated with Delrich Hotels. La Place is ideally located within a few minutes of four of Jersey's most attractive bays – St. Aubin, St. Brelade, Beauport and St. Ouen, and yet is only 3 miles from St. Helier with its evening entertainment and bargain shopping.

La Place Hotel

Route du Coin, La Haule, St. Brelade, Jersey.
Telephone (0534) 44161 Telex 4191462
First Register ○○○○ A.A. ★★★★ R.A.C.

A DELRICH HOTEL

"It is no exaggeration to say that this first class hotel is Bouley Bay and that Bouley Bay is one of Jersey's most beautiful". Ashley Courtenay.

Outstanding natural beauty combines with modern comfort – the result – the Water's Edge Hotel – waiting to provide the most relaxing holiday you'll probably ever experience. A favourite location for visiting yachtsmen, local divers and fishermen, or anyone who likes the sea. Overlooking this centre of marine activity the lounge bar and restaurant are elegantly appointed to provide a background to the life style associated with good living. Outside, a two tier swimming pool, award winning gardens and breathtaking views all add to the magic that is The Water's Edge Hotel.

The Water's Edge Hotel

Bouley Bay, Trinity, Jersey.
Telephone (0534) 62777 Telex 4191462
First Register ○○○○ A.A. ★★★★ R.A.C.

A DELRICH HOTEL

VICTORIA TOWER

Bus route 1, 1a
to Gorey.

A short distance from La Pouquelaye de Faldouet is Victoria Tower. This is reached by walking east from the dolmen down Rue des Marettes for about 200 yards, and then turning left into a private road. You then keep straight on. The tower, together with the approach road and the surrounding heath land was purchased by the National Trust for Jersey in 1980. It was built in 1836, and perched as it is on Mont St. Nicholas above Mont Orgueil Castle, it has a clear view of St. Catherine's Bay.

There is little else on this promontary now, but in medieval days there was a leper house, and during the Occupation, the Germans requisitioned the area as the headquarters of the 2nd Battalion Artillery Regiment 319 and built three bunkers. One had eight rooms and was used as a telephone exchange. The others were two-roomed and served as sleeping quarters for the troops.

GEOFFREY'S LEAP

Bus route 2.

Another National Trust property is Geoffrey's Leap or Le Saut Geoffroi, which is on the sea side of the road leading from Mont Orgueil Castle to Anne Port. The story goes that Geoffrey was convicted of a crime against a woman and was condemned to be thrown over the cliff. The sentence was carried out, but he fell into the sea and swam ashore. There followed a dispute as to whether he should go free, but out of bravado he leapt over the cliff at the same point. By this time the tide had receded and he fell on to the rocks and was killed. A less interesting explanation of the name leap or saut is that before the road was built the accumulated rain from the land above made a waterfall over the cliff. There are excellent views from this spot and as there is a seat it makes a good resting place.

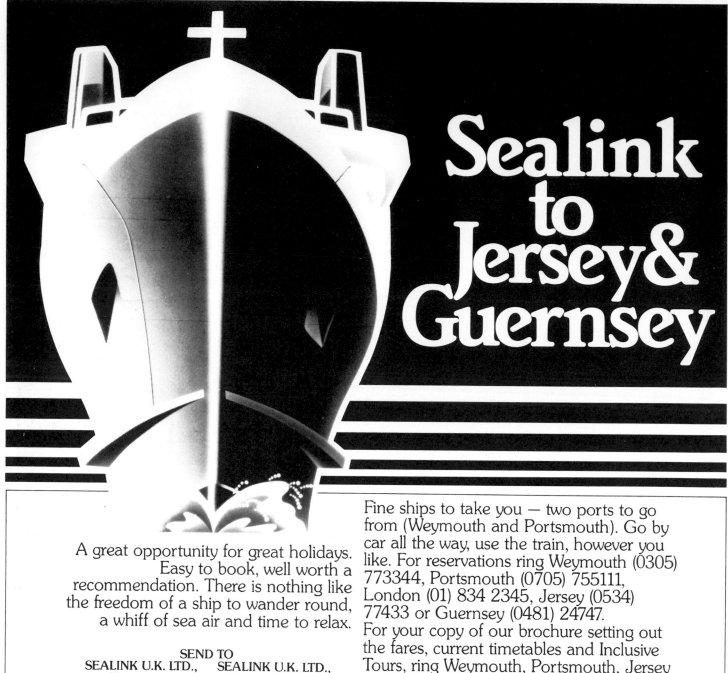

Sealink to Jersey & Guernsey

A great opportunity for great holidays. Easy to book, well worth a recommendation. There is nothing like the freedom of a ship to wander round, a whiff of sea air and time to relax.

SEND TO

SEALINK U.K. LTD.,
Weymouth Quay,
Dorset DT4 8DY

SEALINK U.K. LTD.,
Norman House,
Kettering Terrace,
Portsmouth
PO2 7AE

SEALINK U.K. LTD.,
7 Wests Centre,
Bath Street,
St. Helier,
Jersey
OR

SEALINK U.K. LTD.,
The Jetty,
St. Peter Port,
Guernsey

Fine ships to take you — two ports to go from (Weymouth and Portsmouth). Go by car all the way, use the train, however you like. For reservations ring Weymouth (0305) 773344, Portsmouth (0705) 755111, London (01) 834 2345, Jersey (0534) 77433 or Guernsey (0481) 24747.
For your copy of our brochure setting out the fares, current timetables and Inclusive Tours, ring Weymouth, Portsmouth, Jersey or Guernsey at the numbers shown above, or fill in the coupon below.

Sealink
CHANNEL ISLANDS

Please send me a copy of the current Sealink Guernsey/Jersey Brochure

Name ....
Address ....
....
.... Post Code ....

E.J.

GOREY PIER

Bus route 1, 1a.

Considering the great age of the castle towering above it, Gorey Pier is comparatively recent, having been built in 1820. There was a harbour here long before that, however, as we learn from Dumaresq's survey of 1685 that here was "the most ancient harbour of all in the island" with an "old and decayed pier where such small boats as use the neighbouring coast of Normandy do resort".

The new Quay was built to accomodate coal yards and the growth in the oyster trade. There had long been oyster beds off Gorey which for centuries had been used by local fishermen. At the beginning of the 19th century they came to the notice of English fishing companies and once the pier was built at least 2,000 men were employed, to say nothing of the women who sorted and packed the oysters. Rows of houses sprang up in the village, and Gouray Church was built in 1832 largely because of these workers. Unfortunately the beds in Grouville bay were soon exhausted and these mainland fishermen started to encroach on the French beds of Chaussey which caused a great deal of friction, violence and even fighting. The men were a rough lot, rioting in the village, staging the first known strike in the Island and even raiding new beds laid down by the States to help the industry and not yet ready for dredging. After one such fracas the Constable of St. Martin appealed to the Lieutenant-Governor, who came to his aid with the garrison and the town militia. Unfortunately the Governor himself caught cold, and died a few days later, possibly of pneumonia. This greed and over-dredging soon killed the once prosperous oyster industry and by the mid-nineteenth century only a few thousand tubs a year were exported.

The houses on the Pier were built on land reclaimed during its construction, and in the 1970s the quay was rebuilt to accomodate the frequent passenger vessels from France. Apart from the main harbour of St. Helier, Gorey is the only official sea port in the Island, with its own customs house.

The Eastern Railway was extended to Gorey Pier in 1891 when the promenade was built. Gardens are now laid out on the original track as far as the parish boundary and set in the middle is a fountain which commemorates another of Gorey's industries – that of shipbuilding. For centuries there had been ship-building yards in the bay and the granite fountain depicts the keel of a ship, with the jets of water forming the masts. Underneath is water and around are gardens representing the shore. Along the keel are engraved the names of ships built in these yards, and alongside is an engraved plaque of a fully-rigged sailing ship. A few yards down on the other side of the road is a public garden where every summer bedding plants depict some special shape – perhaps the parish crest, a flag, or the badge of a particular society.

Gorey at turn of the century (G. Amy)

Gorey Harbour

GROUVILLE

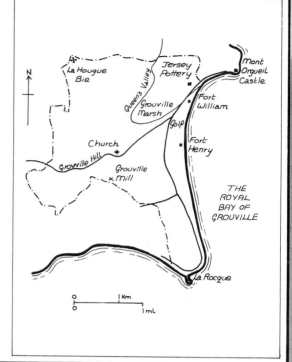

Queen's Valley, beloved by Victor Hugo and George Eliot, is a delightfully peaceful place to walk, and is the most talked-about place in this rural parish as the Jersey New Waterworks Company proposes to create a reservoir there. The stream through the valley once powered three mills: Moulin de Haut, Blanc Moulin (lately the home of television detective Jim Bergerac) and Moulin de Bas, now Lower Mill Pottery where Robert Boissière welcomes visitors to view his highly individual work. The Parish possesses the oldest windmill in the Island whose history can be traced continuously from 1331 and whose tower is preserved as a navigation marker. Nearby is La Croix de La Bataille, the site of a skirmish with the French on one of their early raids. It was probably quite a battle for the old road down to the church from this National Trust property is known as Blood Hill.

The off-shore reef of the Minquiers forms part of this parish, and its granite stone fishermen's cottages are liable to Parish Rate.

GROUVILLE BAY

Bus route 1, 1a

Fort Henry

It was Queen Victoria who, after a visit to the Island in 1859, decreed that this bay should be called the Royal Bay of Grouville. Previously it is thought to have been called La Baie du Vieux Château as Mont Orgueil castle dominates the sky-line to the north. With such a back-drop, all the amenities to hand and good bathing, this beach is ideal for families.

The castle is not the only fortification built to guard the bay. Fort William, now an attractive residence at the northern end, was built in 1760 and was used as a temporary hospital following the skirmish at La Platte Rocque (page 105). The square-towered Fort Henry, situated on the golf course, was built a little later during the Governorship of Sir Henry Seymour Conway (1772-1795) and for a time was called Fort Conway. Six more defensive towers were built round the bay during the Napoleonic wars, five of which still exist. They were sold off by the British Government in 1921.

It will be noticed that the sand is grittier here than elsewhere – a fact that came to the attention of the occupying forces during the Second World War when it was realised that it was the most suitable for concrete production. A 60 cm. gauge railway was built in 1942 and five diesel locomotives, each drawing ten trucks worked six days a week carting the sand either to Gorey Village for collection by lorry or to Gorey Pier where Rhine river barges transported it to St. Helier or St. Aubin. Things intensified in June 1943 when the railway was extended westwards and it was possible to transport the sand direct to St. Helier. Over one million tons of sand were removed from Grouville to be used in practically every concrete construction built during the Occupation, so it is no wonder that the beach level dropped, the seawall (built in 1890) was undermined and the golf course temporarily ruined.

The entire coastline of the Royal Bay of Grouville, with its sandy shoreline, offshore reefs and rocky gullies, provides a rich feeding ground during the winter months for countless numbers of wading birds including curlew, oystercatcher, redshank, grey plover, ringed plover, turnstone and the tiny active dunlin, but of these the oystercatcher is the only species that remains to breed here during the summer when the common tern and sandwich tern will also be in evidence as they breed on the larger off-shore reefs.

The grey heron uses these same reefs as a winter roost and from November until April the bay is a favourite feeding haunt for up to 1,000 dark-bellied brent geese, whose breeding home is far away in the Siberian Tundra.

GROUVILLE COMMON

Bus route 1, 1a

Unlike commons in the United Kingdom this land belongs to the 'tenants du Fief du Roi' – people who own particular houses in the area – and they, therefore, retain certain privileges. For example land for the golf course is merely licensed to the Royal Jersey Golf Club, and it is therefore possible to see an occasional cow tethered near the greens.

Part of the Common is the wetland area behind the sandy heath. This is known as Grouville Marsh and consists of reed and iris beds bordering the stream, damp or flooded water-meadows and scrubland. This small but important stretch of wetland harbours very good numbers of wintering wildfowl, particularly the small but colourful teal, and between a hundred and two hundred common snipe also choose it as a favoured feeding ground. Grouville Marsh is also an important stop-over point for many species of migrating birds during their spring and autumn passage and the area is frequently used by Jersey's bird-ringers. Reed warblers, garden warblers, willow warblers, blackcaps, chiffchaffs and yellow wagtails all pass through the area during their migration to and from their African wintering quarters. In order to preserve this natural habitat for birds and the flora and fauna, the National Trust for Jersey has bought some land adjoining the Common at Les Maltières.

The 71 acres of Common bordering the sea used to be a favourite spot for duels. In 1799 for example, two officers of the garrison fought here and at the sixth exchange of shots one of them, the surgeon of the Regiment, fell dead.

Golf Course

Grouville Marsh

Between the years of 1843 and 1902 the annual horse races were held on the Common. There is a painting by Ouless, which hangs in the Museum, depicting the scene in 1849. These races were a high-spot in the Jersey calendar, with side-stalls and entertainers making the occasion more of a fair than a simple race-meeting. As a girl Lillie Langtry owned a horse – purportedly bought for a shilling, which ran here. Later, when she had gained fame and fortune, she gave another race-horse the same name – Merman. He won the Cesarewitch in 1897, adding to her wealth by £39,000.

Today it is the Royal Jersey Golf Club that dominates Grouville Common. As far back as 1878 a group of local enthusiasts planned the course and some of the world's greatest players have emerged from here. Perhaps the most famous was Harry Vardon who won the British Open Championship five times, but other well-known golfers who received their early training on this course include Ted Ray, who held both the British and American open titles, Aubrey Boomer who was five times Champion of France, and more recently the Ryder Cup player Tommy Horton, who is currently the resident Professional at the Royal Jersey Golf Club.

JERSEY POTTERY

Bus routes 1, 1a, 2
Entrance Free
Open Monday-Friday
9-5.30
Closed Saturdays,
Sundays and Bank
Holidays.
Parking
Restaurant
Suitable for disabled
Guide Book

This is the largest pottery in the Channel Islands, and two hundred different lines (many in several colour ranges) are made and sold on the premises, which are open-plan to enable people to walk round and watch the different processes. Two methods are used for making this pottery – casting and throwing – and hand silkscreen printing is also carried out, mainly on tiles.

It is always fascinating to watch potters at their wheels, but here you can see much more, and with information boards in each studio it is possible to leave understanding exactly how the two methods work.

It is perhaps best to start in the mould-making room where, once the design has been approved for pots made by the casting method, models are made, around which plaster of Paris moulds are formed. From here, the moulds go to the production area where slip (liquid clay) is poured into the mould. This creates a shell of soft clay in the design of the pot, and the next process is "fettling" – the removal of any seams or rough edges. The pots, once dried out, are ready for decorating. Although a set design is followed, all the painting is completely free-hand. This naturally leads to a degree of individuality, and no two pieces are exactly the same. The pots are then sprayed with a glaze, which temporarily obscures the decoration, and are put into a kiln for firing. There are four automatically operated kilns, which heat to a temperature of 1135 degrees centigrade for fourteen hours and then gradually cool for ten hours, giving a twenty-four hour cycle. The glaze becomes transparent during this time and when unloaded the pots are ready for the sorting room and store.

More natural clays are used for the throwing method which produces the heavier stoneware. In this studio everything is made by hand by four potters using wheels. The pots are then fired to a much higher temperature, making the colours more natural.

The pottery, which in the last thirty years has grown from a small family business employing twelve people, is now deliberately labour intensive making full use of the talents and skills of about a hundred local people. Designs change constantly and everything sold in the show-room (apart from accessories such as lamp-shades and candles) is made on the premises. Articles range from a three foot hand-painted stoneware jardinière to the popular double egg-cup. There are also specifically Jersey items such as the traditional milking can and bean crock.

The three and three-quarter acres of garden are as much a feature of the place as the studios, and it is possible to sit and relax in surroundings every bit as colourful as the pottery produced here.

VISIT
The Secret Garden

Tearooms
and Restaurant

Tel:
52999

Open 10.30 a.m.
to 5.30 p.m.

Your visit to JERSEY will not be complete until you have discovered the delights of "The Secret Garden" on Gorey Common where you can tarry a while in a picturesque and peaceful "Old Worlde" garden setting in the grounds of a 150 years old Jersey country house, whilst enjoying the excellent home made fare.

You will be offered a varied choice of quality food including morning coffee, or tea and scones, ploughmans and farmhouse lunches, quiches, crisp salads and paté, gateaux, assorted cakes and fruit pies, and traditional Jersey cream teas, all made on the premises by our own staff.

A charmingly pine furnished dining room is available for use in inclement conditions, so do not be deterred by the weather.

There is easy access for wheelchairs and children are very welcome.

Please, however, be good enough to leave your dogs, other than guide dogs, at home.

LA ROCQUE

Bus route 1

From as far back as the Middle Ages this has been a fishing village, although when the tide is out it might seem highly dangerous to venture into the natural harbour through the maze of jagged rocks that are exposed at low tide. However, there is a narrow channel through which boats can pass safely to reach La Platte Rocque and it was by this channel, Le Canné de l'Orgeon, that the traitorous La Rocque pilot, Pierre Journeaux, led Baron de Rullecourt when he invaded Jersey in 1781.

As La Rocque was the most unlikely place for the French to land the defence was minimal. Even so, the invaders' approach should have been detected. But it was Twelfth Night and to quote from a report at the subsequent court martial of the Lieutenant-Governor Major Moses Corbet, "the Chef de Garde was intoxicated and neglected to fix his sentinel on the battery, which so perfectly commands the shore that no such noise as the landing of troops could escape the ear of any man who was awake." That was not all – no patrols were sent out, and he and his men disobeyed orders by leaving their posts.

The result was that de Rullecourt and his men were able to land at La Platte Rocque (now marked by a plaque) and march into St. Helier (see Royal Square) leaving a hundred men at La Rocque as a rearguard. At dawn the boats used by the French were seen by the troops stationed at Fort Conway on Grouville Common. The young lieutenant in command was horrified to receive orders to surrender from Major Corbet, but eventually a note arrived from Major Peirson with the information that he was going to engage the French in St. Helier, and asking for assistance. These troops from the 83rd Regiment fought the French at La Rocque. Seven of their number were killed and eight wounded, but – as in St. Helier – the French were routed.

Following de Rullecourt's raid the building of defensive towers was intensified. One was built close to La Platte Rocque and, on the islet of L'Avarizon a mile out in the bay, a tower was rebuilt, named Seymour Tower. This is the only example of a square 'Martello' tower in the island. Incidentally, the sea walls at La Rocque are the oldest in the Island and the pier, which is partly on La Platte Rocque, was built in 1881.

Before the Second World War an annual regatta used to be held at La Rocque, where great fun was had by all with events such as barrel races across the harbour.

The tide here recedes two miles, making the vingtaine of La Rocque the largest in the Island at low tide. The temptation to explore the exposed rocks and pools, or walk out to Seymour Tower is great, but so is the danger: the incoming tide races through the gullies and it is all too easy to be cut off. It is advisable to follow the out-going tide and return in good time, before it changes.

LA HOUGUE BIE

There is such a variety of things to see here that there must surely be something for everyone. The name is derived from the Norse word *Haugre* meaning a burial mound and Bie could denote a connection with the Norman family Hambye who once may have owned the site. There is a legend that the mound was built by a Lady of Hambye to commemorate her husband who, having slain a dragon in the marshes of St. Lawrence, was himself killed by a treacherous servant.

The 40-foot mound is, in fact, the most spectacular prehistoric monument in the Channel Islands. Made of earth, limpet shells and rubble it houses a Neolithic passage grave built about 3000 BC. Although it was ransacked, possibly by Viking treasure-seekers, the dry-stone blocking of the passage is intact. It is some thirty feet long, and four feet high and roofed with flat rectangular capstones. The passage opens into the main chamber, two side chambers and a large end-chamber forming a cruciform plan. There is a theory that the centre chamber was a place of worship, with the smaller chambers only being used for burial. This is borne out by the fact that a medieval chapel was built above it in the same way that some parish churches were built on prehistoric shrines, in order to convert the people who flocked to worship there. The great stones used for building the dolmen were quarried from areas several miles away. There is still a mystery as to how these early men, without the invention of the wheel or any mechanical device, could have moved such unweildy rocks from places as far away as Town Hill (now Fort Regent) and Bouley Bay. In fact the whole tomb is remarkable in its design and workmanship, even to the cup-markings which can be seen on the underside of the capstone and the eastern upright of the north side-chamber. The presence of so many limpet shells in Neolithic monuments is a mystery. Were they are offering to some ancient goddess or were they placed to act as a cushion between the cap-stones and the earth above?

Bus route 3a
Price Code C
Open all year
Tuesday-Sunday 10-5
Guide Book

Passage Grave

It is fitting that the Société Jersiaise has its archaeological museum at La Hougue Bie. Exhibits range from flint tools and animal remains dating from the time when man first set foot here during the Ice Age and sheltered in La Cotte de St. Brelade, through to post-medieval pottery and metalwork found during recent excavations in St. Helier. Here too is housed a replica of the Bronze Age gold torque found by workmen in St. Helier in the 1880s. The original, which is now kept at the Museum in Pier Road was probably worn by an important chief about 3,000 years ago. It is four and a half feet long and contains twenty-six ounces of gold.

Archaeological Museum

Guard's van enclosing railway exhibition

Chapels at top of mound

Getting to the chapels at the top of the mound is now both simple and safe. The paths have recently been widened and strengthened so that prams and and wheelchairs can be pushed to the top. From here France seems very close and it is easy to understand how one legend as to how the oldest chapel, that of Notre Dame de Clarté (Our Lady of the Dawn) came to be built: a Norman land-owner disapproved of his daughter's sweetheart, so he banished her to Jersey. Each day she would climb here to try to see her beloved and one morning she had a vision of the Virgin Mary, so she built the chapel. Whatever its origins, this chapel pre-dates the neighbouring Jerusalem Chapel by nearly 400 years. This was built or possibly rebuilt, by Dean Mabon in about 1520 after a visit to the Holy Land. As owner of La Hougue Bie, he hoped to make the mound a centre of pilgrimage and to that end he also built a replica of the Holy Sepulchre underneath the chapels. Note the frescos of angels on the walls above the altar recess in the Jerusalem Chapel.

In about 1780 James d'Auvergne built a pseudo-Medieval tower around the chapels. This became known as the Prince's Tower when his nephew and heir, Philippe d'Auvergne became Duc de Bouillon. This tower was frequented by tourists in the Victorian era "for the panoramic view obtained from its summit' but it was demolished in 1924 when the Société Jersiaise acquired the site.

Down to ground level again, and there is still plenty to see. During the Occupation the Germans built a concrete bunker here to house their communications centre, and this has now been made into an Occupation museum. There is also a railway exhibition within one of the few surviving pieces of Jersey railway rolling stock – a guard's van. Next to this is a reproduction of an old forge with all the original smithy's tools and built with authentic bricks salvaged from a demolition site.

Farming has always played an important role in Jersey, and there is an excellent Agricultural Museum here with a large display of agricultural implements, which benefits from a regular intake of new material from donations to the Société.

There is ample seating in the grounds of La Hougue Bie, so that having explored its various sections, the visitor can relax and admire the surroundings. The mound is particularly beautiful in the early spring when it is absolutely covered with primroses and snowdrops.

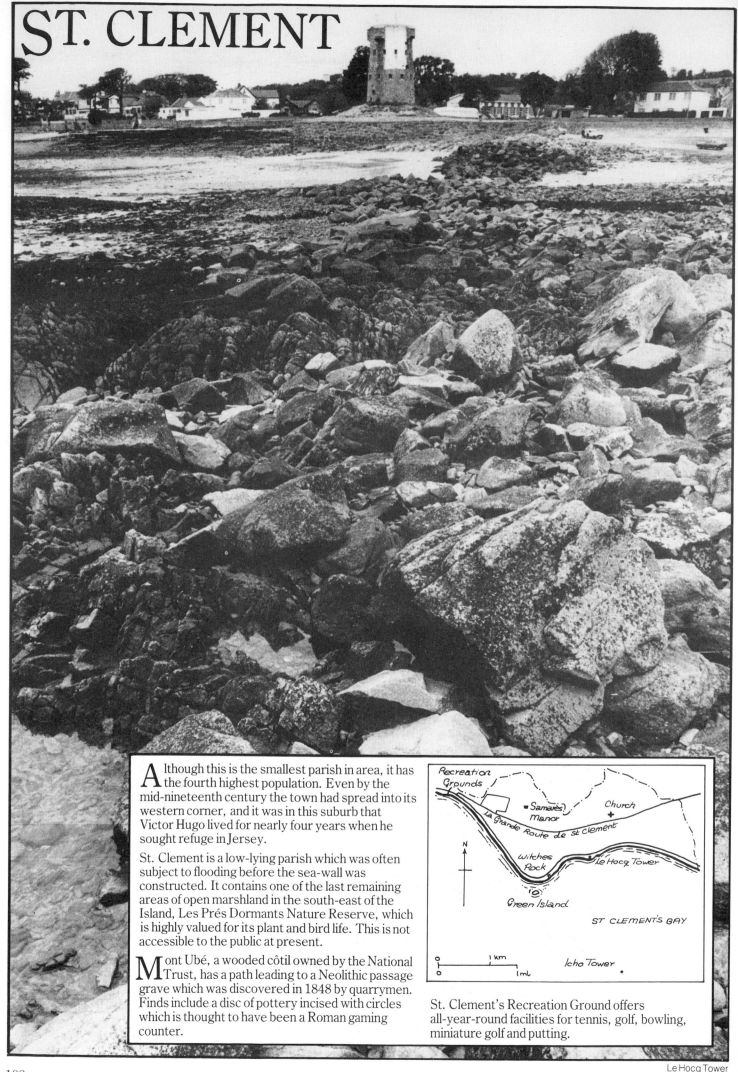

ST. CLEMENT

Although this is the smallest parish in area, it has the fourth highest population. Even by the mid-nineteenth century the town had spread into its western corner, and it was in this suburb that Victor Hugo lived for nearly four years when he sought refuge in Jersey.

St. Clement is a low-lying parish which was often subject to flooding before the sea-wall was constructed. It contains one of the last remaining areas of open marshland in the south-east of the Island, Les Prés Dormants Nature Reserve, which is highly valued for its plant and bird life. This is not accessible to the public at present.

Mont Ubé, a wooded côtil owned by the National Trust, has a path leading to a Neolithic passage grave which was discovered in 1848 by quarrymen. Finds include a disc of pottery incised with circles which is thought to have been a Roman gaming counter.

St. Clement's Recreation Ground offers all-year-round facilities for tennis, golf, bowling, miniature golf and putting.

Recreation Grounds

Samarès Manor

Church

La Grande Route de St Clement

N

Witches Rock

Le Hocq Tower

Green Island

ST CLEMENT'S BAY

1 km

1 ml

Icho Tower

GREEN ISLAND

Bus route 1

This beach, which is the most southerly in the British Isles, is popular with local families. Within easy distance from St. Helier, it has ample parking, sand and shelter. At high tide the bathing is excellent and at low tide the rocks and gullies give plenty of scope for exploration.

Icho Tower (1810-11) is a defensive tower built on an islet about a mile and a quarter from the shore. An iron cross existed there prior to the Reformation giving the islet the alternative name of "Croix de Fer", a name which existed for centuries after the cross had disappeared. It is possible to reach Icho at low tide, but care should be taken that the return journey is started well before the tide turns as it is all too easy to get cut off in one of the many gulleys.

Green Island itself (La Motte) is a tidal islet 300 yards from the shore which was probably joined to the mainland as recently as the beginning of the 17th century. It was here that in 1911 a cist cemetery was discovered with at least fifteen rectangular cists, made from rough slabs of diorite, which can now been seen at La Houge Bie Museum in Grouville. Most contained bone detritus though only four had identifiable skeletal material, one being the remains of a crouched burial.

To the east of the beach, on private land, is Rocqueberg or "Witches' Rock". Forty feet high and with indentations resembling imprints of cloven hooves, this can be seen from the road between Green Island and Le Hocq. This area was once a known meeting-place for witches and naturally several legends have grown up around it. One tells of Hubert, a young fisherman from La Rocque who was lured to the rock by a beautiful nymph. His fiancée, Madelaine, having failed to stop him from keeping the appointment, followed him armed with a Cross. When she arrived, there was Hubert surrounded by evil old women who were dancing and shrieking in mad saturnalia. Madelaine raised the Cross and the witches immediately dispersed. Another story has a similar theme. The witches who congregated there were known to raise storms and fishermen were meant to throw the thirteenth fish from their catch as they passed, to enable them to reach port safely. One day, during a particularly bad storm, a young fisherman cut one arm off a starfish before throwing it and shouted "La Crouée est mon passeport" (the Cross is my passport). As it landed on the rock the storm subsided and from that time the witches of Rocqueberg have not been seen or heard again.

Neolithic graves at La Hougue Bie

SAMARES MANOR

Although the history of this seigneurial Manor is long and interesting, it is perhaps most famous for its beautiful grounds which are now open to the public.

The house itself (lived in by the present owner Mrs Elizabeth Obbard, and not open to the public) has been altered and added to over the years and although there has been a Manor here since Norman times nothing is visible of the original buildings except for the crypt of a 12th century Manorial chapel, dedicated to St. Martha.

What is still standing is the colombier (dove-cot) which is probably the oldest in the Island. This was the scene of an unhappy accident during the Civil War. The Seigneur, Henri Dumaresq, was a Parliamentary leader and when, in 1643, George Carteret captured the Island for the King, he escaped to London – although his effigy was hanged in the grounds. Carteret commandeered the house, first using it as an internment camp for the wives of Parliamentary exiles, and one day in 1647 he sent a certain Mr. Wright to the colombier to collect young pigeons. It seems there was no ladder, for the unfortunate Mr. Wright fell from a great height, breaking his leg and thigh. For two months Madame Dumaresq nursed him at the Manor despite their political differences, but he eventually died.

It was Henri's son who first made the gardens famous, draining the grounds and digging a canal. Later he wrote to John Evelyn: "I have planted a score of cypresses from France and some borders of phillyrea whereof most were from slips. I have this year begun a little plantation of vineyard."

Colombier

South side of Manor

Bus route 19
to Marine Avenue, ½ mile
down La Grande Route de
St.Clement from
Georgetown
Price Code C
Open April-October, 10-5
Closed Sundays
No dogs
Free parking
Suitable for disabled
Refreshments

Herb garden

Successive Seigneurs used the canal to transport them part of the way to St. Helier, but in 1924 Sir James Knott, founder of the "Prince" shipping line, retired to Jersey and bought the Manor. Aided by landscape designer Edward White, and employing forty gardeners, he created gardens that were reputed to be among the most beautiful in Britain. Thousands of cartloads of earth were brought in from every parish to fill the canal and hundreds of rare specimen trees and plants were brought in from all over the world. Many still exist: the Metasequoia (water larch) from Central China, the Ginkgo (maidenhair tree) from Eastern China, the Tulip tree from North America. Another interesting species is the *Taxodium distichum*, a cypress which if grown by water produces woody bumps called "cypress knees" in its roots. There are three at Samarès, but the one with "knobbly knees" is in the centre of the lower pond which was constructed in 1930 as a swimming pool.

West side of Manor from herb garden

The Japanese garden is on an artificial hill made from imported Cumberland limestone, where water falls between the linked pools into the pond below.

These days, with no possibility of forty gardeners, the strategy is one of simplification, with some "low maintenance" areas to allow time to devote to the famous camellia border and the Japanese and water gardens. Rare species are being identified and dying ones replaced, and now there is a new venture – the herb garden and shop.

Of course, the manor would always have had a herb garden, but now 10,000 square feet have been given over to growing more than a hundred varieties. There are four separate sections – culinary, medicinal, cosmetic and dyeing, and fragrant – designed so that people can get close to each herb, smell it and read the label which gives the common name, the latin name and its uses.

The scent is delightful in this walled garden – lemon verbena and rue, lavender, thyme and pineapple sage all giving out their particular smell. Then there's the mint scented alecost, which repels moths, and orris root for making pot-pourri, together with bergamot, rosemary and balm.

The medicinal herbs are of particular interest, especially as these ancient remedies are now given a new credence by the medical profession. Feverfew, for example, is now a popular long-term cure for migraine or one could try purple sage as a gargle for sore throats, heartsease for coughs and skin complaints, sneezewort as a snuff to aid sneezing, or motherwort for female disorders.

At the shop one can buy the plants, dried herbs and pot-pourris and books on the use of herbs.

It certainly is an original concept but one that is in perfect harmony with the lovely old Manor and its magnificent grounds.

Samarès Manor Gardens
HOME OF HERBS-A-PLENTY

The magnificent grounds of Samarès Manor are the perfect setting for Jersey's new venture in herbs and herbalism. Within the 14 acres of landscaped grounds we propagate and grow over 100 varieties of herbs for use in cooking, medicine, cosmetics and dyeing.

The herb garden design is unique : planted in blocks framed by small inter-linking pathways, it allows easy reference to all the species whilst ensuring a fascinating balance of colour, height and texture. The herb shop is always stocked with interesting herbal products, including pot-pourri, herbal teas, dried herbs, cosmetics and herbal remedies. Herb plants are always available, either individually or in attractive potted bowls and there is expert advice on hand on the uses and cultivation of herbs. Enjoy the fine view of the herb gardens while relaxing in our tea garden.

Open April to October.   Admission 85p Adults.   20p Children
There is no entrance charge for those who only wish to visit the shop

Samarès Manor, St. Clement's Inner Road : Tel. Shop 79635 : Estate Office 70551

Get together at Jersey's leading holiday & conference hotel

* Everything under one roof
* Elegant and comfortable surroundings
* Within walking distance of town centre, parks and sea

High class cuisine

The Hotel de France is one of Jersey's leading Hotels, set in it's own extensive grounds with panoramic views over St.Helier. It combines old architectural elegance with modern facilities, catering for all tastes. Residents can enjoy the use of a choice of bars, swimming pool and a new Conference Complex. This complex contains a public cinema, Madisons night club, a de luxe squash club with four courts and a theatre seating up to 720 with top line entertainment. Also situated in the hotel is a sauna/solarium and hairdressing salon. If you are planning a business function, whether it be for a short stay conference of ten persons or a week long gathering of 500 persons, we can provide everything from a simple slide presentation to the latest in cinemascope. Why not talk over your requirements with our Conference Manager Kevin Stuckey.

Hotel de France
ST.SAVIOUR'S ROAD · JERSEY. Tel: 0534 21321 Telex: 4192308

ST. SAVIOUR

St. Saviour has the shortest shore-line of any of the twelve parishes: just Le Dicq slipway, which includes Le Rocher des Proscrits, a rock so named because Victor Hugo and his compatriots used to meet there.

The famous beauty Lillie Langtry was born Emilie Charlotte Le Breton, daughter of the Dean of Jersey, at St. Saviour's Rectory in 1853. She was married twice at St. Saviour's Church: to Edward Langtry when she was 21 and to Hugo de Bathe in 1899. When she died in Monte Carlo in 1929, this society beauty was brought home to be buried in the churchyard where a marble bust marks her grave.

Her birthplace is a private dwelling and cannot be visited. This also applies to Government House on St. Saviour's Hill, which was built in 1817 and became the official residence of the Lieutenant-Governor in 1822.

The western half of the parish is now very much a suburb of St. Helier, giving St. Saviour the second largest population in the Island, but there are still plenty of rural walks, one, Le Val Aumé (Swiss Valley) starts half way down Les Varines and by turning right into La Freminerie and then left into another footpath, can be extended eastwards as far as La Rue St. Thomas.

Les Routeurs – early morning

HOWARD DAVIS PARK

Bus route 1

This is one of several places given to the Island by T.B. Davis, a Jerseyman who made a vast fortune in South Africa, in memory of his son Private Howard Leopold Davis who died in action at Étaples, near Boulogne on August 12th 1916. The park, originally "Plaisance" the former home of Sir Bertram Falle (Lord Portsea) was opened by the Bailiff on 30th September 1939. The Howard Davis Memorial Hall, originally the billiard room, is the only part of the house that remains.

Just inside the main entrance is a statue of King George V – a man deeply admired by Davis who gave an identical statue to a university college in Durban. On either side are two flower-beds, each depicting the emblem of a specific club or organisation. 6,000 special plants are used each year to create these works of art, and credit goes to Mr Larry Goguelin, the park Superintendent who designs them.

The whole park is around ten acres, much of which is laid out as a spacious grass area where people can relax and perhaps listen to one of the many bands that play at the bandstand each summer. The flagstaff, incidentally, is the spinnaker boom from one of T.B. Davis's yachts, the *Westward*.

The rose-garden, which has recently been enlarged, now has 1,400 rose trees as well as a pergola where wisteria adds its own delicate colour. A memorial plaque to James Darling Colledge, who landscaped the gardens, can be seen in front of the lily pond at one end of this garden.

There is another lily pond in the rockery where many species of heather thrive on ground raised by chunks of granite brought from nearby Le Dicq.

In a corner of the park adjacent to St. Luke's Church is a war grave cemetery. This was dedicated on 26th November 1943 and is the resting place of allied servicemen who were shot down over the Island or who lost their lives at sea. Many bodies were washed ashore when *H.M.S. Charybdis* and *H.M.S. Limbourne* were sunk west of Guernsey, and although the occupying force was nervous that it could incite a riot, a funeral was held with full military honours. Hundreds of Islanders attended but it was a time for mourning, not for rioting.

Each grave is marked with a simple oak cross and although the War Graves Commission provided replacement stone tombstones, when their representative saw for himself the dignified effect of the wooden crosses, a decision was made that they would remain in perpetuity.

Although, along with the Union Jack, the national flag of America still flies over this cemetery, the bodies of the American servicemen were removed after the war: a decision regretted both by Islanders and by some of the families who have since visited this tiny cemetery.

Between the cemetery and the formal garden is a large fountain, built to commemorate the Festival of Britain in 1951 and all around are enormous Lombardy poplars which because of their height and age are gradually being replaced with Italian alders.

St. Luke's Church was built as a chapel of ease in the mid-nineteenth century and has an unusual carved altar stone depicting the Last Supper. T.B. Davis provided the church hall – and perhaps he had good reason to remember his family church. He became a ship's boy at the age of 14, and when his ship, the *Satellite,* ran aground off the coast of Norfolk, he volunteered to man the punt in an attempt to save the ship's papers and valuables. The painter broke and he was cast adrift but he managed to survive for thirty-six hours, was picked up by a passing vessel and eventually made his way home. He arrived in Jersey on a Sunday and, taking his place at the back of the church, soon realised that he was attending his own memorial service!

Jersey has good reason to be thankful that T.B. Davis not only lived but never forgot his Island birth-place. The Howard Davis Memorial Park (to give it its original name) is a most beautiful place and, situated as it is so near to St. Helier, many can enjoy its space, its stately old trees, its quiet corners and the mass of glorious colour in its flower-beds.

LONGUEVILLE MANOR COLOMBIER

Colombier

Bus route 2

Le Val Aumé

This colombier (a pigeon house or dovecot) originally belonged to Longueville Manor (now a hotel) and was given to the National Trust for Jersey by the Earl of Jersey in 1970. Although there is a right of way, by arrangement with the present owner of the hotel, the best access is by an entrance at the eastern end of the Manor grounds in La Rue St. Thomas. The path leads through a gate and alongside the hotel – then the colombier will be seen on the right.

The earliest existing record of a colombier at the Manor is in the Assize Roll of 1299, but this present one was built in 1692 by George La Cloche, Seigneur de Longueville after the earlier one had fallen into ruins. He chose this new site to the north of the Manor having obtained permission by Royal Patent which was approved by the Royal Court after a public enquiry. It was said to have been erected "in the garden of St. Thomas", so it is probably near the spot where the Manorial chapel, dedicated to St. Thomas à Becket, once stood and which was probably destroyed during the Reformation. The colombier was restored in 1873 and again by the Trust in 1970, when the cobbled floor inside the building was uncovered.

Colombiers have been mentioned several times in this book and it is interesting to remember how important they were to their owners. Permission to build one was a highly prized privilege and lifted the manor that possessed it high up on the list of precedence. With its hundreds of nesting-holes the colombier ensured its owner a constant supply of food – to the detriment of surrounding farmers whose corn the birds ate. Until the 18th century a tenant's duties included the cleaning of the colombier.

Main Entrance to Longueville Manor

From the main road, look back at the manor. You will see one of the oldest, largest and most ornamental of all round arches in the Island over the front entrance. It is surmounted with the arms of Hostes Nicolle, Bailiff of Jersey from 1560-64. This wicked man, we are told by the Jersey Chronicler, coveted some land owned by a neighbouring butcher. So he had two sheep 'planted' in this man's house, and the unfortunate butcher was subsequently arrested for theft, tried and sentenced to death. As the hangman was putting the rope round his neck the butcher said to the Bailiff: 'I summon you to appear within 40 days before the Judge of the Universe to answer before Him of the injustice caused to me.' And on the 40th day that same unjust Judge fell dead by the wayside as he was returning from the Town.

COASTAL WALKS

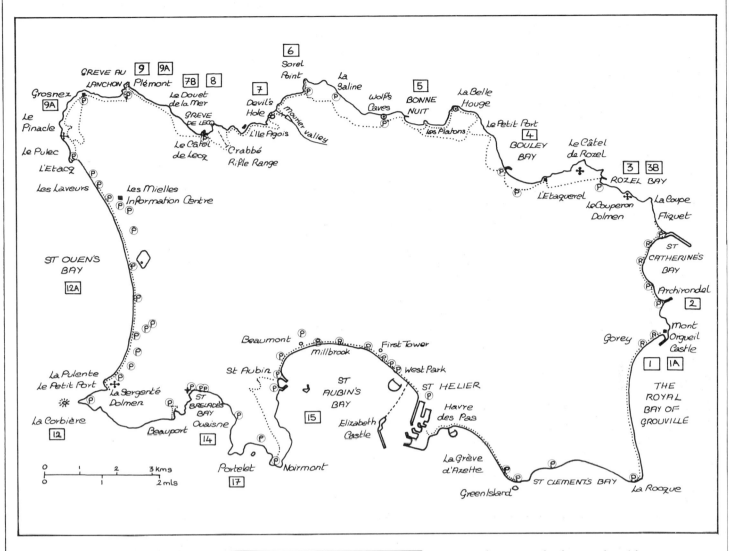

Formal promenades have existed for many years but now, through a local job creation scheme and with the co-operation of many landowners and organisations, new cliff paths have been created so that it is possible to explore much of the Island's unspoilt coastline. Over the coming years the paths are to be further extended so that the scenery, wildlife and coastal fortifications can be more fully appreciated.

Sensible shoes are a necessity on the cliff walks and it should be borne in mind that parts of the north coast path may be too strenuous for the elderly or those of ill health. Keep to the paths, as to leave them could be dangerous or mean that you are trespassing on private land.

A Ⓟ on the map indicates a car park near or adjacent to the footpath. Do not drive in or block fields and farm tracks. Bus route numbers are also shown where a bus service runs to a point along the paths. Consult a J.M.T. timetable for further details.

Vicard Point

118

ST. HELIER -ST. AUBIN

(approximately 3 miles)

The promenade around St. Aubin's Bay, which is illuminated during the summer evenings, follows the route of the Jersey Railway, closed in 1936. At West Park there is a granite pedestal inscribed "Victoria Avenue 22nd June 1897" and it is on this stretch of dual-carriageway as far as First Tower that the annual Battle of Flowers is held. To the west of the causeway to Elizabeth Castle is the West Park Bathing Pool which has a sea-water surface of over five acres. The bay itself is safe for bathing and water-skiing. Things to look out for include the two round towers at First Tower and Beaumont, which used to be much nearer the coast before the land was reclaimed to construct Victoria Avenue, the old railway station at Millbrook, several German bunkers and a strangely short length of anti-tank wall at La Haule, built by the Germans because there was no granite sea wall between La Haule and Bel Royal.

The Promenade from First Tower looking towards St. Helier

Round tower at Beaumont

ST. AUBIN -NOIRMONT/ PORTELET COMMON/OUAISNE

Observation Bunker

Much of the coastline to the south of St. Aubin is private, so it is necessary to go inland before reaching the next stretches of coastal footpath. At the start of the Railway Walk, just past the tunnel, the path divides. The Railway Walk to La Corbière is to the right, but by taking the left-hand fork and climbing a flight of steps, one arrives half way up Mont Les Vaux. It is then necessary to walk on the road to Woodbine Corner and turn left into La Route de Noirmont. Just over half a mile down this road is a cross-roads. To the right is the road to Portelet Common and Ouaisné and to the left is the road to Belcroute Bay. Just past this junction on the Belcroute side is the start of a footpath and bridle path leading to Noirmont. The first stretch is through a delightfully wooded area with such trees as blue cedar and silver birch giving shelter from the wind. This eventually gives way to heather and gorse and views to the east towards St. Helier and Elizabeth Castle and as far as Green Island. Then Noirmont itself, with its German fortifications, its myriad paths and its sheer space is reached (see page 44 Noirmont). By returning to the crossroads mentioned above, by any of the many paths, a left turn will take you to Ouaisné. This road divides before long, and the left-hand fork leads to Portelet Common. These areas and the next stretch of coastline are described on pages 42/3 (St. Brelade's Bay).

It is now possible to walk from St. Brelade's church, round Bouilly Port and up to Beauport. A path from the car park at Beauport leads to a promontory with fine coastal views and at present a fishermen's track provides limited access along the cliff towards La Corbière.

THE WEST COAST
(3¾ miles)

La Sergenté

This stretch of coastal walk begins from the little beach of Le Petit Port and skirts round the promontory of L'Oeillère (the blinker). At each end there are paths (private but with right of access) leading to the headland above, which not only offers

marvellous views of La Corbière and St. Ouen's Bay, but also the chance to see the earliest tomb in the Island. La Sergenté, which can be found by heading towards the housing estate and then turning to the right, is a circular tomb built around 3,700 B.C. at the beginning of the megalithic era. The roof was once corbelled and resembled a conical hat. This is the only tomb of its kind in the Island.

At La Pulente the path continues along the length of St. Ouen's Bay to Les Laveurs Slip. A guide to this footpath can be obtained from the Les Mielles Information Centre at Kempt Tower. (Also see St. Ouen's Bay section of this book on pages 55-60.)

LE PULEC -PLEMONT
(approximately 2 miles)

A steep climb just west of the Lobster Pot restaurant leads to Les Landes, the windy north-western promontory of the Island (page 63), and the path passes many German fortifications, Le Pinacle (page 67) and then through the wetland area of Le Canal Squez from where, over the centuries, purple moor grass has been cut and used

View from Lighthouse at Grosnez looking East

Caves at Plemont

for making milking stools. Other rare plants in this area include cotton-grass, lesser skull-cap, and marsh St. John's wort. The Glanville Fritillary, a rare British butterfly, breeds here. The rifle range and the racecourse are kept to the right and eventually Grosnez Point, with its castle and lighthouse, is reached. Here are perhaps the finest views of the other Channel Islands – and a chance to return to Le Pulec by a circular route.

By keeping to the cliff-path one passes a concrete platform, not a relic of the German Occupation as it existed before the war, but possibly something to do with a signal station which was once there. Soon there are good views of La Grève au Lanchon, Sand Eel Beach – so named because of the sand-eels caught there. All round this part of the coast there are many caves, some of which can only be entered from the sea but others, such as La Cotte à La Chèvre (which is known to have been used as a shelter for Palaeolithic man about the same time as La Cotte de St. Brelade), are accessible from the land. On reaching Plémont there is a path to the beach where several more caves can be explored. This is a delightful bay, but swimmers should be warned not to swim too far out because of dangerous currents.

PLEMONT -GREVE DE LECQ
(2 miles)

Greve de Lecq Beach

Apart from superb coastal views, this stretch affords some excellent vantage points for watching several species of local breeding seabirds. Small colonies of puffins and razorbills nest each year on the inaccessible cliff faces below the Plémont Holiday Village, and although numbers have decreased over the past fifty years, they can still be seen in the early morning or evening, flying to and from their nesting burrows or swimming and diving for food close inshore. The fulmar petrel is another breeding seabird of this area, and although at first glance it can be confused with the common herring-gull, the characteristic gliding on stiff grey wings makes it easy to separate the species. A cliff ledge nester, the fulmar is a comparatively new breeding species to the Island and is steadily increasing in numbers.

Just before reaching the wooded côtil that leads up to Le Lecq Farm, it is possible to reach Le Douet de la Mer, a pretty cove with a water-fall, a cave and an island. After the woods, the coastal path follows the road until it drops down into Grève de Lecq. From the path there are good views of this popular bay, with its coarse yellow sand which is used to purify the Island's water supply. The pier, which has been recently rebuilt, was originally constructed in 1872 and partially destroyed by a storm thirteen years later.

Puffin (Stentiford)

Greve de Lecq Pier

GREVE DE LECQ -DEVIL'S HOLE
(2½ miles)

Path to Devil's Hole looking West to L'Ile Agois

Devil's Hole

The Devil

From Grève de Lecq the coastal path follows the road to the north of the Barracks (see page 72). On the left is Le Castel de Lecq, a natural eminence some 270 feet high which was probably used as a hill fort during much of the Iron-Age. One clue that it was used as a refuge in medieval times is found in an account of Pero Niño's raid on Jersey in 1406. Jerseymen taken prisoner at the Battle of the Dunes at West Park told Niño that "there were five strong castles in the Island". These could well have been the two castles at Gorey and Grosnez, Le Chastel Sedement in Trinity where most of the Islanders took refuge, Le Câtel de Rozel and Le Castel de Lecq. The construction of the guard house in 1779, the use of the mound by the Germans during the Occupation and continuous cultivation have eroded the earth-works but nothing, except perhaps the difficulty of the climb, can detract from the marvellous views from its summit.

Le Castel de Lecq

Our route now leads behind Crabbé Rifle Range, but soon one emerges on the promontory of L'Ane, under which is another fine cave. Very soon L'Ile Agois, a tidal stack separated from the mainland by a narrow gorge, comes into view. Access to L'Ile Agois is difficult and is possible only at low tide by descending the cliff, crossing the rocky beach and climbing the south-west face. This should never be attempted after rain as the bed of a stream joins the path to the beach. A cave, the gulley and a natural arch can all be explored at sea level, while on the summit of the stack are the remains of two roughly oblong structures and as many as 27 D-shaped depressions. In two archaeological surveys carried out in 1974/5 (details of which can be found in the 1979 Annual Bulletin of the Société Jersiaise) archaeologists Margaret Finlaison and Philip Holdsworth put forward the theory that these could well be the remains of a monastery for Christian hermits. Although the evidence is not conclusive, a Charter of 1042 calls the parish church of St. Mary "Sancta Maria arsi monasterii", which implies the existence of a burnt monastery, of which there is no other record.

The cliff walk continues between high hedges to Le Col de La Rocque, a National Trust property where traces of ancient sheep runs are still visible. From here, especially at sunset, there is a good view of Devil's Hole, originally called Le Creux de Vis (Screw Hole) – a view somewhat marred by the concrete viewing platform erected round this blow-hole for safety reasons. The walk to The Priory Inn is completed by road, and a detour can be made down to the platform past *the devil* whose origins date back to 1851 when a French cutter *La Josephine* was wrecked in the area. The ship's figurehead was washed into the hole and the owner of The Priory, Nicolas Arthur, paid a sculptor to add arms, a trident, horns and a tail, thereby giving the new name to Le Creux de Vis. The present "devil" is a replica as the original was burned by hooligans claiming to be the Ku-Klux Klan.

DEVIL'S HOLE -SOREL

(1½ miles)

This walk starts on the headland to the north-east of Devil's Hole, and leads down into Mourier Valley. This was once one of the most deserted and beautiful places in the Island where the stream turned three water-mills and plunged into the sea as a waterfall. Today the valley is used by motor-cyclists for scrambling, the stream is dammed by the New Waterworks Company and its water pumped into Handois Reservoir, and the one relic of historical interest is the remains of Jersey's first knacker's yard at the northern most part of the valley.

Having climbed to the other side of the valley, the view across to Sorel is magnificent. The different colours of granite in the cliff face add interest and the walk is always, to say the least, invigorating. There is a lighthouse at Sorel, which is the northernmost tip of the Island and offers glorious views over the dangerous Paternoster Reef to Sark, while to the east can be seen the massive workings of Ronez Quarry. Between Sorel and Ronez, at half-tide level, is Le Lavoir des Dames or Fairies' Bath. This is a large rectangular hollow in the rocks which appears to be man-made – but for what possible reason? Legend has it that if any man sees fairies bathing here, he will be struck blind.

It is necessary to walk along the road until the next stretch of the coastal path starts at La Saline (the salt-pan). This road is not without interest, as it was made by people forced into unemployment during the German Occupation. When the Labour Department were faced with 2,300 men without work, it was suggested that this road be constructed so that the men would not be made to work for the occupying force. Given the name "La Route du Nord" it now has a stone at one end inscribed "This road is dedicated to the men and women of Jersey who suffered in the World War, 1939-45".

La Route du Nord

Stream in Mourier Valley

Mourier Valley

LA SALINE -BONNE NUIT

(1 mile)

At the start of this walk it is important to look beyond the Resources Recovery Board site towards the headland of Cotil Point, as this is an area of unique importance to geologists. It is the only place in the Island which shows the relation of the different types of granite to one another and of the granites to the volcanic rocks. At low tide one can also see a raised beach formed many thousands of

Wolf's Caves

years ago, when the sea-level was about 25 feet higher than it is now. The walk leads round the headland and soon there is a steep stepped path down to Wolf's Cave which is 350 feet long, 60 feet high and from 20 to 50 feet wide. It is reached via a narrow concrete path at the foot of the cliff. However it should be remembered that he who walks down must climb up again, and the path can be dangerous, especially in wet weather.

Fremont Point, above Bonne Nuit, offers yet another memorable view, and in the springtime the gorse adds its own touch of colour and smell. There is a prehistoric earthwork on the promontory which could well have been of a defensive nature. Apparently amongst the older inhabitants of the neighbourhood, the point is known as Le Châte, or the Castle. Steps bring the walker down to the road leading to the bay.

Raised Beach

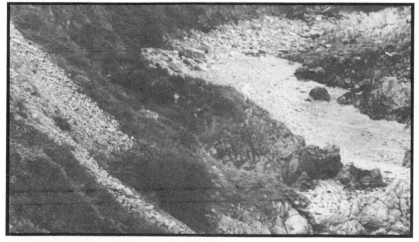

BONNE NUIT -BOULEY BAY

(4½ miles)

This walk starts just past the Cheval Roc Hotel, and there is a choice of a lower and an upper path on the first stretch, which is useful for those without the time or energy to venture further. The next bay around from Bonne Nuit is Giffard Bay, sometimes known as Dead Man's Bay as the rock on the eastern side, Le Long Êtchet, looks very much like a prostrate body. The beauty of La Belle Hougue has already been extolled on page 80 and the next stretch of path is one of the prettiest, especially in the spring when wild daffodils (Lent lilies) flower in abundance. Very soon the path drops down into Le Petit Port where, on Christmas Day 1943, nine men led by Captain Philip Ayton, carried out a Commando raid code-named Operation Hardtack. The raid was intended to provide details of enemy positions and to take prisoners, but ended with little success and with the death of the 22-year-old leader who trod on a mine as they were leaving. In fact the path these brave men took, and which we now follow, leads by the now deserted farm of Egypt. This was abandoned by the owners because the guns at Batterie Mackensen to the north of St. Martin's Church used to fire directly overhead towards La Belle Hougue. The area was then used as a battle training ground by the Germans, who sealed it off.

When the path divides there are two alternatives: the right-hand path leads via Les Camps du Chemin to Les Platons and so back to the cliff path to Bonne Nuit, while the path to the left leads to Bouley Bay. Having climbed up through the wooded area one is again on the cliff-top and this time the view stretches right across the bay to Le Tour de Rozel. The path leads past La Pierre de la Fételle, a stone some 15 feet by 13 which some think resembles a fallen menhir while others feel that it is a fairy stone with special powers, especially at Hallowe'en.

Further along can be seen the remains of a guard house, and then the path becomes a grassy track and leads inland, winding down to Bouley Bay.

Top: Bouley Bay from the East. *Bottom:* Cliff path East of Bouley Bay

BOULEY BAY -ROZEL

(2¼ miles)

This stretch of coastline can be reached either from Bouley Bay, by steps leading past the Water's Edge Hotel, or from the eastern end of La Commune du Fief de Diélament, which is ablaze with yellow gorse in spring and purple heather in summer. After crossing a stream, there is a climb to La Tête des Hougues – a National Trust property given by the children of Captain John and Clara Starck in 1960. L'Etaquerel Fort, built in the 18th century as a defence against the French, and added to in 1835, soon comes into view and the path passes its well-preserved powder magazine. To the east and west of the Fort are areas which were medieval sheep-pens and when one reaches the area below the Côte du Nord Hotel, it is important not to stray from the path as there are two very deep blow-holes in the vicinity. There is an exit to this part of the cliff path leading on to La Route de Rozel, but the path continues another half mile to Le Câtel, where one can see all that remains (200 yards or so) of the great earth rampart, Le Castel de Rozel.

Jardin d'Olivet looking towards Rozel

THE EAST COAST -ST. HELIER

Although the north coast offers the finest cliff walks in the Island, it is, of course, possible to walk right round the coast-line. The path to Le Couperon dolmen described on page 95 can be taken to La Coupe, and there is a new stretch of path from Flicquet to Archirondel, an area described on page 91 (2 miles).

From Castle Green at Mont Orgueil Castle one can descend the steps to Gorey and walk the length of Grouville Bay (page 101 to La Rocque. For those dedicated to complete a round-the-Island walk, the next stretch has to be undertaken either along the road or, with difficulty, along the rocky beach at low tide, but once La Grève d'Azette is reached there is a promenade, with an equally inviting alternative of the long sandy beach.

The promenade at Havre des Pas, past the outdoor swimming pool, is the route of a German railway from Grouville Common (for the transportation of sand) and for the final 'leg' there is a choice. One can walk up the hill, passing Bramerton House on the right, where T.E. Lawrence, better known as Lawrence of Arabia, stayed as a child, and through La Collette Gardens. Here can be seen La Collette House, once the Royal Engineers' Barracks and more recently the office of the Lieutenant-Governor. Alternatively, to keep to the coastal path, one can walk round to La Collette, with the electricity power station towering to the right and the vast fuel storage containers to the left. A short walk enables one to see the Harvey Memorial and the Westaway Memorial. These stand side by side and the first is to the memory of Captain Henry Beckford Harvey and the gallant crew of the *Normandy* which collided with another vessel in thick fog in 1870. The captain and fourteen members of his crew sacrificed their lives to save those committed to their care. Alongside, the Westaway Memorial commemorates the gallantry of John H. Westaway, a passenger who displayed great courage during the same disaster.

To end the coastal walk though, why not retrace your steps and climb Mont Bingham, named after a former Lieutenant-Governor, by the narrow path just past the power station. From here one can enjoy truly spectacular views of the harbour, St. Helier and the indomitable Elizabeth Castle.

Promenade at Havre des Pas

La Collette House and Gardens